Praise for Rob E

"I am so glad to have this oppor~ ~~~~ ~~~~ greetings and congratulations to Rob Bryant. Rob's determination certainly is an enormous inspiration. George joins me in sending our very best wishes."

—Barbara Bush

"Congratulations on your accomplishment of a cross-country trip on a RowCycle. That was a monumental achievement, and I wish to congratulate you on both your mental and physical endurance. I deeply admire what you have done!"

—Arnold Schwarzenegger

"Rob is a coach's kind of guy; he never quits. Rob set two world records even though he is paralyzed from the waist down. He is a man of faith, and I am looking forward to walking with him in heaven some day."

—Tom Landry

"Rob Bryant is an effective speaker! He had our staff laughing one minute and crying the next. He is an inspirational man who, by example as well as a very effective presentation, is able to give encouragement and hope to those who have the privilege of listening to him. He will be a hit with your group."

—Zig Ziglar

"Rob, I am overwhelmed by your accomplishment in the face of unbelievable obstacles! You are worthy of the highest praise for motivating millions of people to improve their health and fitness."

—Kenneth H. Cooper, M.D.
author and aerobics authority

"Rob believes that we should never give up! God has given us the ability to either accept our situation, or change it."

—Joni Eareckson Tada

"The next time you moan about twenty minutes on an exercise bike, think about Rob Bryant, who finished a four-month, 3,280-mile workout on an oar-equipped tricycle. . . . Though paralyzed from the waist down, he also pushed and pulled himself with braces and crutches over twenty-four miles from Fort Worth to Dallas! Both of these are world records!"

—Ben Brown, *USA Today*

WALKING THROUGH ADVERSITY

7 Steps to Overcoming Life's Challenges

ROB BRYANT

Health Communications, Inc.
Deerfield Beach, Florida

www.hci-online.com

Library of Congress Cataloging-in-Publication Data

Bryant, Rob
    Walking through adversity : 7 steps to overcoming life's challenges /
Rob Bryant.
      p.   cm.
    Includes bibliographical references.
    ISBN 1-55874-914-4 (pbk.)
      1. Suffering—Religious aspects—Christianity. 2. Success—Religious
aspects—Christianity. 3. Bryant, Rob, 1955- I. Title

BV4909 .B79 2001
248.8'6—dc21

                                            2001024738

Publisher: Health Communications, Inc.
            3201 S.W. 15th Street
            Deerfield Beach, FL 33442-8190

Cover design by Andrea Perrine Brower
Inside book design by Dawn Grove

This book is dedicated to some of the important women in my life: my wife, Wanice; my mother, Dorothy; my mother-in-law, Janice; my sisters, Kay and Kim; and my grandmothers, Ina and Olive.

CONTENTS

ACKNOWLEDGMENTS

There are too many people to thank for their support, but allow me to acknowledge the encouragement of the hundreds of organizations I have spoken to and that encouraged me to document the stories, accomplishments and adventures in this book. A special thanks to my pastors: Paul Burleson, Michael Dean and the late Hal Brooks. I also appreciate my stepmother, Jane, who would not rest until I finished this book. Her encouragement and input were invaluable. I want to thank Allison Janse, the HCI editor who discovered me through my Web site; Christine Belleris, Erica Orloff and Mary Ellen Hettinger, the talented editors of this book.

Thanks to my family and friends without whom my world records could never have been achieved.

Thanks to the art department at Health Communications, for their talent and creativity: Larissa Hise Henoch, Lawna Patterson Oldfield, Andrea Perrine Brower, Lisa Camp, Anthony Clausi and Dawn Grove.

INTRODUCTION

Fire is the test of gold;
adversity, of strong men.

—Seneca

What Is Adversity?

My personal walk with adversity happened as it does for many of us: totally unexpectedly, and very suddenly. In a split second, in the middle of an ordinary workday, I fell fifty-five feet and was left physically paralyzed. No longer able to effectively move my legs or feel anything from my waist down, the course of my life was changed forever in that one horrific moment.

I left for work a healthy, muscular husband and father of one, with another baby on the way, and was airlifted away a paraplegic. However, I have since learned that this was not the end of my life, but the beginning of a new one. Although I will never run with my children like other dads, or dance with my wife the way I used to, the accident was a transforming experience that led me down a totally unanticipated life road—and to a closer walk with God.

Since that fateful day when I was told I would never walk again, I have set one World Record for walking twenty-four miles on crutches, and set one Guinness World Record for rowing 3,280 miles across America, while raising more than $10,000 for charities, including the American Paralysis Association. I was mentioned in the *Congressional Record* twice, received a certificate of recognition from the President's Council on Physical Fitness, and received congratulatory letters from governors, generals and movie stars. The flag of the United States was flown over the Capitol in my honor and I've written three books.

Today I'm proud to say that I'm the vice president of Quality, Assurance & Compliance for DynCorp, a very large aerospace company. Even more importantly to me, I have two wonderful children and a beautiful wife, and we're a very happy family. And, although I was a follower of Christ, I now understand on a much more personal level that God's promise to be with us always is irrefutably true.

With His help, and my determination to set and achieve what doctors called my "impossible" goals of walking again, I have learned that nothing is impossible. Moreover, I believe part of my purpose and part of God's plan is to help others learn that they, too, can achieve the unattainable. If you are depressed, there is hope. If you are seriously ill or disabled, you can live each day with joy. Each of us has it in us to triumph over tragedy.

At some point in our journey on this earth, each one of us will have to face adversity. It can either make us better—like fire tempers steel—or it can break us. I define adversity as any obstacle—physical, emotional, situational or spiritual—that stops you along your life's walk. My walk through adversity began twenty-five years ago, when I was left wheelchair-bound from a fall.

If you are facing adversity in your life, such as an illness, the pain of losing a loved one, living with children who are out of control, etc., you can't just get up and walk out of your "wheelchair" either. Adversity just does not leave because you wish it away.

However, if we face the pain head on, we can walk *through* it. We can grow from it. We can learn from it. We can not only walk through adversity, we can be stronger because of it. While my physical paralysis happened in an instant, emotional, physical, spiritual and intellectual adversities happen just one nerve at a time. Each time we quit, learn a new fear, say no to God or succumb to our weaknesses, we are slowly beaten by adversity. Soon, we can't move, we can't feel and thus have inadvertently allowed adversity to paralyze us.

Because I can't physically feel sensation in my legs and hips, I can be seriously injured without realizing it. Years ago, for example, I received second-degree burns from the knees down from scalding water and was completely oblivious to this fact for hours—until I looked down and saw the blistered skin. As one of my doctors explained it, "Pain is your friend! It tells you when something is wrong." You must experience the pain before you can take appropriate action.

However, just like my body didn't allow me to feel the burns, your body may not be letting you feel your pain. You may be ignoring it, working it away or medicating it away. Yet each time it comes back, it constricts you more, until you, too, can't move.

On the other hand, there are times when my brain automatically tries communicating with my legs. For instance, when waking up from a deep sleep, I sometimes try to jump out of bed just like I used to do. Then I remember I am a paraplegic and can't do that anymore. One day not long ago, I had to move quickly out of the way of an oncoming truck. I instinctively tried to stand up and move. Within half a second, my brain remembered my legs don't operate that way any longer, and signaled me to take alternative action. Fortunately, I pushed my wheelchair out of the way just in time. While adversity stops some people from moving, others realize they must steer a new course for themselves by a different set of actions.

I meet so many people who have allowed adversity to stop them emotionally, intellectually or spiritually. Because they are difficult to be around, they have fewer friends and their problems are exacerbated.

Conversely, you can grow from adversity, learn from it and allow it to mold you into a better person. Many of the world's best athletes, scholars and leaders overcame personal adversity to become experts in their field. For instance, when Lance Armstrong became stricken with cancer, naysayers predicted his cycling career—and his life—were over. However, with the support of his family and friends, a determined and faithful Armstrong overcame his cancer, in a large part by riding *through* it, and went on to win the Tour de France.

Because of my physical disability, I see life through different eyes than most. Besides seeing life from a much lower perspective—three-and-a-half feet tall (my height in my wheelchair)—I can see other people's disabilities. We all have disabilities of some sort, our own personal challenges we have to overcome. I have also learned that my own physical disability is not nearly as damaging as the greatest disability: the dreaded "I can't" disease. If you suffer from this crippling disease, you're right: If you think you can't, you can't. This disease receives satisfaction from losing a fight, and declares to the host person, "See, I told you you couldn't do it." The "I can't" disease is only one of the many forms of adversity described in this book—and for which I offer cures.

How Can This Book Help You?

As a paraplegic, obviously my ability to walk with braces and crutches and set world records didn't just happen. These accomplishments required thoughtful goal setting: first setting small goals leading to larger ones, and following through at every step, regardless of the considerable pain. I am not saying that every one of us will successfully reach every goal we set, or that we will never fail. Failure is a part of life. A reporter asked Thomas Edison how he was able to invent over fifty useful items for people, including electricity. He replied, "By inventing thousands of items, most of which are useless." In other words, if you attempt ten goals and only achieve five, you still accomplished more than you would have if you hadn't tried.

In an earlier book, I documented my struggle to walk again in an effort to encourage others. Several readers told me that the same method of setting small steps at a time leading to my goal, steps that I used to walk again with crutches, helped them overcome a problem they were facing. Intrigued by this, I again relied on these same steps in other areas of my life. Sure enough, they worked, whether the problem area was physical, mental or spiritual. I spoke with friends about these steps. They used them, too, to beat many types of adversity. Over the course of ten years, I further developed these steps to make them helpful to others facing adversity of any kind.

Part One of this book shares my personal story of overcoming adversity, and Parts Two and Three outline the principles by which I live and my goal-setting techniques. You may be thinking, "That's fine for him, but he doesn't know my problems." However, each of us can approach problem solving, accomplishing goals or overcoming adversity in the same way, regardless of the nature of the goal. The doctor uses a scalpel whether he or she is removing an ingrown toenail or performing heart surgery, because it's a tool that works.

It is my hope that this book provides you with the tools you need to overcome the adversity in your life and the knowledge that there is no challenge so great that it cannot be overcome. That is God's promise to us.

PART I

My Own Walk Through Adversity

Chapter 1

My Fall
to Grace

Are not two sparrows sold for a penny? Yet not one of them will fall to the ground without your Father knowing. Even the hairs of your head are all counted.

—Matthew 10:29–30

The Fall That Took It All

The day I am about to describe to you changed my life. A precious part of me was taken away forever. The date was December 10, 1982. By 7:00 A.M. we were on location at Cat Canyon in southern California close to Santa Maria. I was working in the oil fields as a production logging engineer. Suddenly, the cable that lowered the tools down into the well jumped out of its pulley on top of the portable mast truck. We were in trouble! The mast could not be laid down because the cable was fed through a tall piece of pressure equipment. The company representative was growing impatient and did not want to stop injection into the well, which left only one thing to do. One of us had to go to the top of the mast unit and put the cable back into the pulley. This was not a particularly dangerous procedure, and most of us had done this before. Three of us discussed our options. The safest and fastest way to correct the problem was to hoist one of us up to the top of the mast unit on a cable attached to a winch. Now the question was, who was going to go? I reluctantly elected myself, since I had the most experience and was the crew supervisor that day.

Very carefully, I secured the lifting device around my hips.

One of the other men began the winch that lifted me slowly into the air. Within seconds, I was fifty-five feet in the air and directly across from the pulley. At my command, the winch man stopped lifting me. I tried to fix the pulley, but the cable could not be forced back into the sheave. Try as I might, it wouldn't go. I decided to take the sheave off and take it down with me—perhaps it could be repaired. Unfastening it, I put it in my lap. Suddenly, I felt a jerk. I looked up at the pulley holding me. It was tilting sideways at a funny angle. Looking down, I saw how high fifty-five feet really was. Realizing the danger I was suddenly in, I decided I wanted down quickly.

"This pulley up here looks strange," I called down to the hoist man. "It might not—"

I felt another jerk, only this time I wasn't stopping.

"Oh God, I'm falling! Somebody help me!" I screamed as I began to plummet. Everything seemed to go into slow motion. *This can't be happening! I'm in a bad dream,* I thought to myself in horror.

As the ground rushed up to meet me, I remember praying that God would kill me then and there. I knew if he didn't, I was going to be very badly hurt. Well, God didn't, and I was. I landed in a sitting position, hitting the ground with my rear. My backbone broke with a sickening and audible crunch while I was still in the sitting position. Next my back and head slammed down on the ground. Whatever I hit with my head caused my helmet to fly off and my skull hit as if against cement. My ears rang with the sound of the impact and crack-ing bones. I felt a tremendously painful sensation in the middle of my back as if someone had stuck a knife into it. Everyone came running over to me. Never losing consciousness, I was in a state of shock as the horror of my fall and excruciating injuries began to dawn on me. Suddenly, I realized I could not feel anything from below my stomach down. Breathing was painful and very difficult, as the stabbing pain in my back affected my lung capacity. With every gasp of air, my back hurt even more. I spit broken teeth and blood out of my mouth. Blood was also trickling down the side of my head into my ear.

Slowly, my reasoning returned and I looked around. Directly over my chest was an iron fence that ran around the well head. That's what I had hit my head on. If I hadn't been wearing my helmet, the fence could have broken my neck or caved my head in. Looking directly up, I saw something that no one who witnessed the accident has ever been able to explain. My body was not lying directly beneath the broken pulley that had caused my plunge. Instead, I was approximately six feet over to the right of the well head. If I had fallen straight down, as gravity dictated, I would have been impaled on the pressure equipment and killed instantly. But I wasn't.

Considering what had just taken place, my thoughts were fairly clear and I was all too conscious of the pain and the dire situation I was in. But the voices of the crew around me were distorted and distant, as if I were in a tunnel. One of the men used his radio to call the office, which called the hospital. But as the minutes passed by, the pain in my back grew worse. I tried moving my legs. It was no use; they wouldn't respond. I couldn't lift my head, but I could turn it slowly. I could move my fingers, but my arms felt too heavy to lift. I looked over at Dave, one of the operators. He was looking at me with disbelief in his eyes. Slowly, the shock of the fall dissipated and the grim reality of the situation began to sink in. I could not feel or move from the waist down, and I was over an hour away from the nearest hospital.

"My God, my back is broken," I said out loud.

"Rob, the paramedics are coming. Just hold on. You're going to make it," Dave said, with a tone that wasn't very convincing.

"Dave, what do I look like? I can't feel my legs. Are they still there?"

"Yes, they are there. I'm not going to lie to you. Your left foot is bent sideways. It's probably broken, but the rest of your body looks okay. How do you feel?"

"Like I've just fallen fifty-five feet," I said in a weak attempt at sick humor. Even the halfhearted chuckle I managed caused severe pain to shoot through my entire abdomen. I stopped right away. My internal organs felt like they were torn to pieces. And breathing was more difficult.

After a few more minutes of gasping for air and feeling tremendous pain, I prayed out loud: "God, help me! I'm not going to make it."

Suddenly, breathing was easier, but the pain grew worse. It seemed like hours before I could hear a siren off in the distance. At first, it was far away and faint, but it rang louder and louder until it pulled into our location and paramedics raced over to me. The lead paramedic was very proficient. By asking me a few questions, he knew what had to be done and the probable extent of my injuries. His voice sounded much clearer than Dave's had been just minutes before.

"What is your name?" he asked, looking into my face.

"Rob."

"Rob what?"

"Rob Bryant."

"Where are you?"

"On a well site running," I took several breaths, "a production log."

"Where do you hurt?"

"My back."

"Can you feel your legs?"

"No."

"Can you turn your head and move your fingers?"

"Yes," I said, showing him.

"Okay, just lie perfectly still. We are going to put you on a stretcher and prepare you for a helicopter."

"Please be careful. I feel as if I am broken in two."

Not Ready to Die

They began removing the chain that was wrapped around my hips. My boots were cut off and pants slit up the sides so they could look for further injuries. I was lying in some water and for the first time, the sixty-degree air and steady breeze began to make me shiver. Each and every vibration hurt my back and I was becoming sick to my stomach. I prayed I would not cough or vomit.

Before I knew it, they applied a splint to my broken ankle and placed me on a stretcher. They put a sheet over me to keep in my body heat. I was awed at their efficiency, and if I weren't in so much pain, I would have told them. Talking was too much of a strain on my back and lungs as I lay there at their complete mercy.

"Please, God, kill me. I can't stand any more pain," I whispered. One of the paramedics heard me.

"I don't want to hear any more talk like that. You're doing really well. You can make it. Don't give up."

"Can you knock me out with a painkiller?" I asked, gasping for air.

No such luck. The paramedic explained that, since they didn't know the extent of my injuries and because my head was bleeding and I might also be bleeding internally, it was too dangerous to knock me out just yet. He urged me to just "hold on" and said I was "doing really well."

Doing well? Who is he trying to kid? I remember thinking. As I lay there, wondering if I would die, I made three quick decisions that today I am absolutely convinced saved my life: I wanted to see Wanice and Jason again; I wanted to live long enough to see my new baby that was due in thirty days and hold that baby in my arms just one time; and I wasn't ready to die!

"God, I know I am asking for a miracle, but give me thirty days of life. Let me live long enough to tell my family good-bye and to let my new baby know that Daddy loved him—or her," I whispered through the tears and excruciating pain. In my thoughts I'd had an ongoing dialogue with God, begging him alternately to let me die or let me live. But now I knew I wanted to live.

The pain grew worse. I began moaning with every breath. I just couldn't get enough air. I lost consciousness for about five seconds, but the immense pain revived me. I have heard of people dying of pain. Now I can believe it!

I was relieved when I finally heard the distant whir of the helicopter, but my relief was to be short-lived. As it landed, dust and dirt blew everywhere, filling my nose and mouth. The agonizing pain in my back was momentarily eased as they lifted the stretcher and carried me smoothly to the chopper.

But I weighed 230 pounds and I know the paramedics felt every pound. Then they discovered I wouldn't fit into the helicopter on the stretcher! I was too tall for the compartment.

"Take the door off!" the pilot yelled over the roar of the engine and prop. He turned to me and yelled with a smile, "This will be just like Nam."

If he was trying to make me feel at ease, it wasn't working. They removed the door and shoved it in behind me. Instead of letting my feet hang out of the open door, they let my head hang out. One of the paramedics jumped in with me and away we went. The sound was deafening. The added G-force exerted on my body as we took off almost made me pass out. Suddenly, I found it even more difficult to breathe because air was rushing by my head hanging out in space. The air whizzed by at an incredible speed, forming a near vacuum over my nose. Each breath was a near impossible task, but I refused to give up. I fought the fear of suffocating. "Oh, God, help me breathe," I prayed yet again. I forced myself to just take one breath at a time. If I worried about the next breath, I would panic and suffocate for sure, I felt. Finally a paramedic glanced over and saw me struggling desperately for air. He cupped his hands over my face, allowing me to breathe freely again. As the frigid air bathed my wet body, I was freezing—at least the parts of me that could register sensation were. I was shivering, trembling and my teeth were chattering all at once from the cold and shock. Each involuntary wave of shivering was felt in my back and along my spine, hurting beyond words. I was torn between wondering why I hadn't passed out, feeling cheated of the oblivion of unconsciousness, yet afraid that if I did go out cold I might never open my eyes again. I was struggling, second to second, to survive.

Several minutes later, we landed at the Santa Maria hospital. You've seen it all on TV: Hands pulling the stretcher from the chopper, paramedics briefing doctors and nurses as they raced across the helicopter landing pad on a gurney. I heard voices yelling "Grab this" and "Stabilize that" until I was set carefully down on a table in the emergency room. If I hadn't been paralyzed, I'm sure they would have had to scrape me off the ceiling, because as soon as my swollen vertebrae hit the table, I screamed with pain. What a scene that was: As I was screaming virtually with each breath, doctors shaved and stitched up my head while simultaneously grilling me about what I was feeling and the accident and could I feel my legs. A nurse asked me questions about my wife and son to make sure they were not losing me. In the background, I heard somebody say, "Fifty feet! My God, I wonder what his insides are like." I was in too much pain to worry about dying at this point—I went back to relishing the thought of being pain-free—forever.

Still without any anesthetic or painkiller, it was on to the X-ray department where I was placed on another hard metal table, which pushed relentlessly up against my broken back. I wondered how much more pain I could take, and for the first time since the accident, I cried. I found out later that my broken vertebrae were pushing out almost through the skin. (Since that experience, the pain is seared into my brain and to this day the thought of another X ray still makes me shudder as I flash back to the nightmarish day of the accident.) After several X rays of my back and skull, I was told to wait to see if they were going to develop properly.

"I'm not going anywhere," I jokingly told the X-ray technician through the tears. Finally, after an excruciating twenty minutes on the X-ray table, I heard the magic words.

"Mr. Bryant, I'm about to administer an anesthetic. This should relieve you of the. . . ."

Those would be the last clear words I would hear for over a week. It had been almost six hours since I plummeted from the winch—undoubtedly the longest, most painful hours of my entire life.

In the meantime, Wanice was notified of my accident. She left Jason with a neighbor, and a friend picked her up a few minutes later. All she was told was that I had fallen and that I was hurt. She was not told the extent of my injuries. Once she got to the hospital, she had to wait for over an hour in the waiting room for a report. Finally, the doctor came out of the emergency room to talk with her.

"Mrs. Bryant, at this point we don't know how serious Rob's injuries are. This is what we do know. He has a broken back and ankle, internal bleeding, and is experiencing paralysis from the waist down. What we are most concerned about now is controlling the internal bleeding. Also we do not hear any bowel sounds, which is very serious. At this point we have no way of telling how much damage has been done to his spinal cord. If it is not bad, he will experience almost total return of his leg movement. If it is badly damaged, the paralysis may be permanent. I have scheduled a surgery tomorrow morning for your husband. I am going to straighten his backbone, insert two steel rods on each side of his vertebrae and fuse it all together. The next forty-eight hours will tell us how serious his injuries are. I don't believe in pulling any punches. I feel I have an obligation to tell you the truth. I hope I have not shocked you."

As Wanice told me much later, at this point she just went numb. Her husband had left home that morning a healthy, physically fit man. Now he was fighting paralysis and quite possibly for his life. At eight months pregnant and with a young son at home, Wanice said she felt as if this was more than she could bear. Somehow she made it through the first few days with the help of our friends. However, two weeks later, when the full reality of the horrible situation finally set in, she broke down and cried for days. But I was not aware of this at the time. Wanice was determined to keep me from seeing her pain, knowing that it was all I could do to concentrate on the battle that lay ahead of me.

Surgery, Drugs and Pain

My back surgery began at six o'clock in the morning and lasted until three o'clock in the afternoon. Wanice and a few of my coworkers came to the hospital during the surgery, but I didn't reach even semiconsciousness for several days. The only thing I remember of the first week is occasionally waking to hear Wanice's sweet voice reassuring me that everything was going to be all right.

On one such occasion, I had the following experience in a semidream state.

The darkness was the thickest black I had ever seen. Slowly, the darkness dissipated into a dull gray. I began to be able to make out sounds: "Beep. Beep. Beep." I could hear voices off in the distance. I started making out forms of people standing around me. My eyes focused on the shape closest to me. A doctor was wrapping me with wet strips of white bandages. He was winding them completely around me. He appeared to be making a mummy out of me. I couldn't move, lift my arms or talk. I looked around the room. I was surrounded by equipment that was beeping and blinking. A tube ran up my bed and disappeared into my nose, down my throat and into my stomach. My throat was raw from trying to close as I swallowed or coughed. My mouth was so dry I would have killed for a drink of cool water. Another tube, which catheterized me, ran up the bed. There were several electrode monitors placed on various parts of my body. A large intravenous bag was suspended over my bed with a tube that ran down to a needle in my left arm. The doctor continued to wrap me with long wet strips of cloth. By now I could see he was making a plaster cast around my upper body from my lower waist up to my armpits. I was being suspended above my bed by some sort of apparatus, which allowed the doctor to wrap the strips all the way around me. One of the nurses produced a needle and gave me a shot into my IV. Slowly I faded out again.

I faded in and out of consciousness for days. Somehow, despite the morphine, I remembered my granny's phone number. I knew if I could just hear her voice, everything would be okay. In my dreams, I was back walking around in her garden as a child. Reaching over to the phone with a great deal of pain, I managed to dial her number. A loving voice answered the phone.

"Granny, this is Rob."

"I know your voice, Rob."

"Granny, I have been in a terrible accident."

"I know, Rob."

"Granny, I want to live."

"I know."

"Granny, I want to walk."

"I know."

"Granny, will you pray?"

"Rob, you know I will."

"Granny, do you know those stairs going up to your front porch?"

"Yes."

"Well, Granny, you and I are going to walk up those stairs in just a few months."

"I believe it, Rob," she said as she began crying. Hearing her tears, I burst into tears myself.

"Rob, it's a date. Your Granny will be here waiting for you," she promised.

We talked for a few more minutes before I hung up. My family told me later that she prayed for several days with very little sleep, food or water. I owed my life and what was about to happen to Granny's loving prayers. She told my uncle, "I am going to pray until God gets tired of hearing my voice and answers my prayer."

Meanwhile, I was painfully aware of the body jacket I would wear for the next three months. Since it was rock hard, it hurt my back and made it very difficult for me to breathe. Slowly, I was weaned off the stronger drugs, but my back pain grew worse. Sleeping became impossible in the plaster body jacket. I couldn't move because of its size and weight. About every four hours I was rolled to a new position, but I was in pain after just a few minutes. I thought the physical and mental stress would drive me mad.

On the tenth day, I was moved from intensive care to a semiprivate room, which was not occupied. They thought it best that I be alone since I was experiencing hallucinations and paranoia from the drugs, and I would scream as the drugs

wore off and the pain escalated. The isolation made my situation worse. Wanice could not travel much in her condition, so
she visited about every third day. I felt as if God, my wife and
my fellow workers had abandoned me. Slowly, the drugs and
pain decreased. I began to think more clearly, although I
resisted calling relatives or friends because of the deep depression that came upon me along with a return to full consciousness. The shock of the accident passed, and I was left more
clearheaded to face the grim reality of my situation. I was a
paraplegic!

Now that I was becoming much more aware of my surroundings, the body jacket was even a bigger problem. I was
sliding down into it. My raw back was sliding across the rough
interior, and the jacket began to rub against the incisions from
the surgery. I told several of the nurses it was bothering me,
but they were so used to my screams they just chalked it up to
me being a complainer. The plaster cast actually rubbed my
surgical incision raw before they finally took me seriously and
fixed it.

Soon it was Christmas Day, and Wanice brought Jason to
see me. It was the first time I could remember seeing him
since the accident. Jason was two and a half years old and
couldn't understand why Daddy couldn't walk. He wanted me
to come down on the floor and play with his toys with him.
It was certainly nothing like the Christmas I had imagined
having just a month before. Jason got on my nerves very
quickly—I just was not myself emotionally—and our visit
was cut short. Several of my other friends from church
stopped in, but I didn't want their company for very long
either. Besides a broken back, I was struggling with a broken
spirit. Everyone who visited, including my firstborn son, was

just another cruel reminder of the permanency of my tragic situation and of what I would no longer be able to do. I had been through tremendous physical pain and now was facing the cruel reality that I may never walk again. This was not something I could medicate away with drugs.

Chapter 2

The Prayer

Let your light shine before others, so that they may see your good works and give glory to your Father in heaven.

—Matthew 5:16

Lord, I Don't Understand

On December 31, Wanice made her final trip to see me before she would fly home to Texas to have our second child. It was the most difficult separation we had ever known. She did not want to leave me all alone in California, and I needed her by my side. A couple from our church, Bob and Ruth Peterson, brought her up to Santa Maria. What can anyone say at a time like that? They had no idea what to say to ease our agony at parting. The three of them visited with me for a couple of hours. When it was time for them to go, I asked one of the nurses if I could be transferred to a wheelchair to escort them to the door. The nurse had to get permission from a doctor because I had not been "released" from the prone position. The doctor allowed me to take a short trip in the wheelchair. After a twenty-minute struggle, I was in the chair. This new position made me sick to my stomach, and I thought my back was breaking, but I knew I had something important to do. I insisted on pushing the wheelchair on my own. The four of us went downstairs. As we were on our way to the door, we passed the room I had been told about; it was the chapel.

"Wanice, Bob, Ruth, I have some business to take care of in the chapel. Would you like to join me?"

We entered the beautiful chapel from the back. There were stained glass windows and an ornately covered altar in the center. We went up to the front pew where we all sat down. By now my back was killing me, but I knew what I was about to do was the most significant thing I had done in years. I turned to my visitors.

"I need to talk to the Lord, and I wanted you to be here. Let's pray," I said as we all bowed our heads. It grew very quiet.

"Lord, I don't understand why all of this is happening to me, but I am going to seek you and your will. I pray that something good will come of all of this. As I read the Bible, so many of your people didn't understand why they had to suffer either. Job, for instance was a godly man, yet you chose to let him suffer for a long while. I have read that story, and I want the end of that story for my life. You totally restored him in the end. God, please do this for me. I promise I will give you all of the praise and glory for anything I accomplish."

After I finished, it was deathly quiet. The only sound was Wanice's muffled sobs. She was dreading having to leave me, and knew she'd be giving birth to our new baby without me by her side. Then a real miracle happened. Within seconds, the bitterness I was fighting inside, the kind that some people live with for years or a lifetime, just vanished. After this time, I would still have occasional bouts of discouragement, but the bitterness was gone. Even though my back hurt beyond words, I was comforted inside where the lasting pain would have been. Bob and Ruth began to cry with Wanice. We left the chapel and I rolled to the door to say good-bye. No one knew what to say, so we just hugged, and they walked out of the door. For the next six weeks, other than God and an occasional visit from friends, I was alone.

Just after Wanice left, I called Jim Hurst, a friend in my Sunday school class back in Texas. We talked for awhile and then I said the words that would change my life: "Jim, whatever it takes, I am going to walk back into my Sunday school class. I know it is impossible, but just you watch."

He said, "Okay," but I could tell he was just trying to be nice.

*   *   *

On January 6, I was flown to Downey, California, on a small care-flight to begin my grueling four months of rehabilitation in another hospital. Now that my condition was stabilized and I was healing, there was nothing else the hospital at Santa Maria could do for me. The trip was very painful. I felt every pocket in the air and every bump on the road.

The rooms didn't have phones in them, so I arranged to have one put in for the big day: the day that our new baby would be delivered via C-section. I woke at 4:00 A.M., and the minutes and hours crept by. I hoped I could have started my therapy right away in order to keep my mind occupied. I felt so left out knowing Wanice was having our baby so far away, and I couldn't do anything to comfort or help her. It bothered me that I had to hear about the birth of our second child by phone instead of being there, as we'd planned before the accident. It also bothered me that I would not see the baby for two weeks after its birth. Everyone was there, it seemed, but me!

At nine o'clock my phone rang. My stomach was up in my throat. *Had everything gone okay? Was my wife all right? Was my baby healthy?* I answered the phone.

"Hello, is that you?"

"Yes," came a tired, weak voice from the other end. "I

wouldn't let them put me under sedation until I could tell you what we have. Rob, we have the most beautiful, precious little boy you have ever seen. He is healthy, and I am okay, just a little tired and sore. I love you, Rob. I can't wait to see you and show you our little boy, Jonathan. I've got to go now. See you soon."

"I love you, too. I'm glad you and Jonathan are fine. Thanks for being so strong," I said, not sure she heard or understood me in her condition. She handed the phone to her mother, and we talked for awhile. After she hung up I was so excited, even though it still saddened me that I could not be there.

At ten o'clock, Ruth Peterson and Judy Wilson walked in my room to celebrate Jonathan's birth. I told them Wanice had already called and told them all of the news. I tried to hide my frustration and was fairly successful. They seemed just as excited about the birth of my son as I was. They hung a little sign over my bed that congratulated me on his birth. Judy and Ruth and their husbands were becoming regular visitors and we were growing very close. We talked and prayed together for awhile. We thanked God for His grace in answering our prayers and giving us another healthy child. I tried to be as cheerful and thankful as I could, but it wasn't working. Finally, knowing I wasn't fooling them with my mask, I broke down and cried. They cried right along with me. It was during those moments that we grew even closer. Today I'm convinced that God had sent these people to be with me during that time.

Just then, a young doctor entered the room and said, "Excuse me, ladies, but I need to speak with Mr. Bryant for about ten minutes. You can just wait in the hall," he said politely.

"We'll be right back, Rob," Ruth said on her way out of the room.

After they left, the doctor closed the door and turned back to me. "May I call you Rob?"

"Certainly."

"Well, Rob, I just wanted to welcome you to Rancho Los Amigos. It is standard practice for a staff doctor to examine incoming patients to ascertain the neurological damage level. We need to determine your situation before we can come up with a plan for your rehabilitation here. I am going to ask you some questions and perform some simple tests. First of all, can you move either of your legs at all?"

"No," I responded quickly.

"Try. Can you lift them, roll them, move a toe or anything?"

"I can't, but I'll try," I said as I began trying to move my legs. The doctor finally stopped me just short of the point where I was about to turn blue with effort.

"Okay. That answers the question of movement. Now, let's test your sensation level. We'll try what we here like to call the pizza-cutter test."

"What in the world is that?" I asked.

"This should answer your question," he said, reaching into his smock pocket. He pulled out an instrument that really did look like a pizza cutter, except it had tiny spurs instead of a cutting wheel.

"What are you going to do with that?" I asked, hoping my suspicions were wrong.

"I need to know where the sensation level begins in order to make an estimate of the paralysis."

Before I could say anything else, he matter-of-factly pushed the pizza cutter over my left leg. Starting with my left foot, he then proceeded up my calf, past the knee and onto my upper thigh. I could see the white dimples it left on my skin so I knew he was touching my leg, but I couldn't feel anything. The tiny indentations disappeared after just a second. I wondered, *If I could feel sensation, would it hurt?* My question was soon answered when he got to my lower waist and I yelled, "Okay, I can feel it now."

He stopped the test and jotted down some notes on his clipboard. "That was very good. Now let's try the other leg."

What did he mean by "good"? I wondered. He repeated the process on the other leg until he got to my lower stomach on my left side.

"I can feel it now!" I yelled again.

He wrote a few more notes, and then, looking up, he apparently noticed the sign Judy and Ruth had put up about my brand-new son's birth.

"A boy, huh? That's great," he said as he paused, as if he had something more to say. "I have something to tell you, but I'm not sure this is the time."

"Go ahead, doctor, I think I know what you are going to say."

"What I am about to tell you is not an absolute truth, but it is a strong indication of what you should expect." He paused for a second. "Do you remember taking the pizza-cutter test two days after your accident?"

"No, did I have one?"

"Yes, I've got a record of it right here. You were probably so sedated you don't remember. According to the previous record of the test, and judging by the test I just did on you here, there has been no change in your motor or sensory abilities since your accident. And as of today, it's been one month since your injury. Based on these tests and the fact there have been no noticeable signs of improvement, I have an obligation to tell you something. "Rob, in all probability," he paused, took a deep breath, and closed his eyes before saying those words that will forever ring in my ears, *"You will never walk again."*

Despite the fact I was expecting this news and had tried to prepare myself as much as possible for it, I was still shocked.

"But a doctor at the Santa Maria hospital said there was a chance that my feeling and movement would return," I said in disbelief.

"That's correct, but normally if you are going to have any appreciable return of sensory or motor abilities, it would have already taken place by now. You see, every day that goes by, your chances of regaining movement or sensation are greatly lessened. In fact, statistics tell us that if a person is not moving anything from the waist down after thirty days, he or she most likely never will regain any movement or use of their legs. Based on this, most of the therapy we'll give you here will be based on helping you to live your new life in a wheelchair, not trying to walk again. I'm very sorry."

The doctor paused and looked back at the sign over my head about Jonathan, and he struggled for something else to say to me.

"Congratulations again on the birth of your son," he muttered as he turned to leave. I felt sorry for him that he had to deliver such a terrible message to a perfect stranger. How many times a week did he have to utter those words, "You will never walk again"?

I wasn't sure what to say either, so I just answered, quite cockily, given the current state of affairs: "Thanks, but I've got news for you. My newborn son Jonathan and I are going to learn to walk together."

I'm not sure where those words came from. They just

popped out of my mouth. He winked at me and then left. His words still rang in my ears—*You will never walk again.* Up until that very moment, I really believed—or perhaps I had just been desperately trying to convince myself—I could almost completely recover.

❖   ❖   ❖

Three days later, they moved me into a different ward where I would begin my rehabilitation work. My home for the next three and one-half months was Room 518, bed one. The room was approximately twenty-five feet across by twenty-five feet wide and had three beds on each side. Except for the many pieces of medical equipment, the room reminded me of my military days in the barracks. I realized right away that my roommates had been there for some time. Pictures were hung over each bed, and each guy was very possessive about his personal space, little as it was. I shared the room with five other men with spinal injuries. During that time Mike, Max, Donnie, Stewart and Grant would be my family. We learned to encourage each other and laugh and cry together.

My first two days were spent in bed just being introduced to the staff of doctors, physical therapists, occupational therapists, nurses, aides, recreational therapists, a social psychologist, a few of the hospital directors and other residents.

But, while the professionals were planning my rehabilitation process, with typical stubbornness I had already made my own decision: I was going to work as hard as I possibly could to learn to stand and walk again. In fact, the first thing I would talk to my physical therapist about was using braces and crutches. In anticipation of this weighty discussion, I prayed constantly for two days. I was convinced that God would help me, too, if I was willing to do my part. I vowed to give Him all of the praise and glory for my accomplishment.

First things first: I had to sit up and get used to being in a wheelchair. A nurse dressed me in loose clothing over my cumbersome body jacket, including a diaper the size of a small blanket. I felt like Baby Huey. Next, a large tarp was slid underneath me, by rolling my body in the plaster cast from side to side. Then the nurses moved a small hydraulically powered hoist over to my bed and hooked the loops at each corner of my tarp to the long lifting arm. As I gritted my teeth in fear, they slowly pumped the hand lever to raise me up in the air over my bed. Then they carefully rolled the hoist away from my bed and positioned my slightly swaying body over the wheelchair below. Having lost all faith in mechanical means of lifting after the accident, I was truly terrified that the hoist or tarp would break or split. But I was lowered slowly and safely into my chair.

Next I was belted in with a seat belt, since I couldn't use my legs to stop myself if I began slipping out of the chair, or tipped and fell. My body cast pressed down on my thighs so hard that they started to turn white in this sitting position. Then I began to feel lightheaded and sick to my stomach, since this was my first time in the chair in over a week. My longest stay in the chair up to this point had been just an hour. With my determination to learn to walk in mind, I couldn't wait to work up to just sitting a little each day. I set my goal to stay in the wheelchair that day for two-and-a-half hours. Although the nurses obviously thought my goal was a little unrealistic, they agreed to let me try. My back began hurting the moment I was placed in the chair, but I wasn't going to say a word. I had set a goal to walk into my Sunday school class and I was going to do it! Lying in bed was not going to get me anywhere.

I rolled the chair over to the low sink to shave and brush my teeth, but I practically scared myself into jumping out of the wheelchair. My hair was a greasy mess, I needed a shave and I was as white as a ghost—I'd been so focused on survival that my appearance hadn't once crossed my mind. I did what I could, but the only thing that would help this mess was a long, hot bath. I would soon learn the hospital was understaffed at night, and I would only get one or two baths a week. After brushing my hair into an Elvis Presley-style hairdo, I rolled down the hall to work with my physical therapist for the first time. On the way there, I stopped at the nurses' station and spoke with a few of them. They encouraged me to give therapy my full attention. I agreed I would. Understandably, many of the patients who passed through this rehabilitation hospital were not in a terrific mood at the time and consequently made life difficult for the nurses. But I knew that my paralysis was my problem, certainly not the nurses' problem, and I decided I would try to be a blessing to them. All the while, of course, I thought that I was going to beat this thing.

Upon rolling into the physical therapy room, I saw many strange pieces of apparatus. The "racks," as they were called, had several victims in their clutches. The patients had their legs lifted or spread at radical and painful-looking angles. Elsewhere people were trying to transfer out of their chairs onto a table of equal height. There were tables with suspended pulleys for leg exercises, for those who could move their legs. A cart with all sizes of dumbbells was in a corner. A rickshaw-like apparatus was in the middle of the room.

Weights were placed behind the patient on the ends of the long sticks with a fulcrum in between. The patient would push down on the sticks to work on triceps and chest muscles. At the far end of the room were wall pegs with braces and crutches hanging down, as well as a set of long parallel bars. A patient named Mike was trying to walk with braces between the bars. I rolled down to watch him for a minute. I could see right away that he had some voluntary movement of his legs. He could straighten his thigh some, but he had no movement from the knees down. Braces on his calf and ankles kept them straight and extended. I watched him carefully because, as I told myself, *This is what I'll be doing in just a couple of weeks.*

Not a Good Start with the Therapist

I heard my name being called from behind me. I turned and saw the physical therapist who had been assigned to me, waving me over to where she sat at one of the tables.

"Hello, Rob. I'm Beth. How are you feeling?"

I told her I was fine and anxious to begin therapy.

"Good. The first thing we are going to try is the transfer from the wheelchair to the mat."

"Okay, but later I want to talk to you about trying to walk with braces like that man over there," I said, pointing to Mike working on the parallel bars. She turned to look at him and then turned back to me.

"Well, let's not get too far ahead of ourselves. Mike is much younger than you are and he can move his legs; you can't.

Maybe I'll let you try that in the future if I feel you can. But try to be realistic. You'll only be disappointed if you build up unrealistic expectations."

"But I've already decided I am going to walk," I said, smiling. "Just you wait and see." She was silent and shot me a stern look as her face reddened. I felt as if she had taken my statement as a personal affront to her authority and expertise.

She then answered, "I am your physical therapist and I am in control here. I will say when you are ready. Now let's get back to business. You will transfer yourself from the wheelchair to the mats."

"I didn't mean to make you mad," I said, stunned at her reaction, but determined to get beyond it. "It's just that I've set a goal to walk. I thought you would be excited about that! I won't bring it up again." Maybe she was just having a bad day.

She regained her composure and handed me a long, skinny board to slide on in order to scoot across to the mat. I slipped it under my rear and tried to slide to the mat. But because the plaster cast couldn't bend, I couldn't push down enough to lift my rear off the mat. I finally made it after three attempts.

"Now slide back into your chair like this," she said in a dull tone, demonstrating how to transfer in the reverse direction. After about fifteen minutes of sweat and effort, I plopped back into my chair. After five weeks of being in bed, my formerly muscular arms were weak and shaky.

"Now do it again," she said, as she walked off to help someone else. I was so exhausted and almost out of breath, but I was going to make sure she saw that I was prepared to work.

"I'll give it my best shot," I told her with determination in my voice.

During the following hour, I completed four more transfers.

I couldn't believe this little bit of exercise was taking so long and wearing me out. I was in the process of trying one last transfer when Beth returned, said I could go and then walked off again. Another therapist who'd noticed how hard I had worked told me that I had done really well. *Why couldn't Beth give me a pat on the back or a little positive reinforcement?* I wondered.

Finally, my two-and-a-half hours in the wheelchair were over and I headed back to my room. Although my back was in a lot of pain by this time, I ate sitting up for the first time since my accident five weeks before. I felt almost normal for a change, and I didn't have to worry about spilling as much. After lunch, I was put back into bed with the hydraulic lift. Sitting had caused deep bruises to bloom on the top of my legs from the body jacket, though of course I couldn't feel the soreness.

As the first few weeks passed, I spent more and more time in the wheelchair, for hours at a time. Then came the day that I tolerated eight hours of continuous sitting. This is when my therapy increased in its ferocity. Now, not only was I in a transfer class at nine o'clock, but I then went on to lift weights, do endurance training, take "wheelie" class, and do ranging and dressing sessions.

Weight lifting consisted of using dumbbells and a pulley apparatus to work on my arms and chest. It felt good to work out, but I was inhibited from going all-out by my back pain. I started with a fifteen-pound dumbbell that felt like fifty. The pulley system was a little better; I could pull sixty pounds. I also practiced "dipping" with the parallel bars. I put my feet into a strap that was hung between the bars and then tried to lift my body weight several times. This was very difficult and painful inside my body jacket, with my legs being dead weight, and with a still-painful lower back. At first, I couldn't manage more than ten raises.

Next, I started on the endurance track in the wheelchair to increase my lung capacity and help me maintain a strong cardiovascular system. Now that my activities were severely limited, weight gain and the loss of strength were constant challenges that required daily attention if I was to overcome them. The track was approximately one mile. A physical therapist timed each lap around the track in the wheelchair and checked my pulse before and after to record any improvement. Because I knew walking was going to be even more tiring eventually, I worked extra hard. I began trying to dress myself in the mornings, but I couldn't reach my lower legs or feet until the body jacket came off. Beth came to my room once a day to "range" my legs. This was necessary because the muscles start to tighten up and contract without any movement. Ranging consisted of a one-hour torture treatment on a rack to stretch my legs. The ranging was complete, it seemed, when the therapist had wrapped your legs around your head and body four times in a knot. While being molded into a human pretzel would be painful for most people, it was excruciating for me due to the hypersensitivity in my legs. Hypersensitivity is caused by severed nerves that can't carry normal sensory impulses. Instead, they send distorted pain signals in which even the slightest touch feels like an electric shock.

With little more than five weeks to go in the rehabilitation center, I thought it was time to approach Beth about the prospect of walking again. She immediately said "No!"

"What do you mean, no?" I asked with disbelief.

"I mean," said Beth, "your injury is so severe you will never use your legs functionally again for walking. Your insurance company will not pay for the additional weeks in the hospital if there is no real hope of you ever doing it. It takes that long to teach you to walk with braces and crutches. I told you before you can't walk unless you have some leg movement. I have been through this before with other patients. I know you want to walk, but that is impossible in your condition. You're just going to be terribly let down. Besides, I would be wasting my time when so many other people just need my time for basic skills. I know you are excited about walking, but I have much more experience than you when it comes to this. I am not going to go through the time and expense to do something I know is useless. My decision is final."

"Beth, if I don't try, how will I know if I might have walked again? Just being able to stand up using braces would be a big boost to me, psychologically. And the exercise can't hurt. Besides, the biggest reason I've got to try is that I've promised my Sunday school class that I was going to walk in some day. I can't just give up without trying."

"The answer is still no! I am your physical therapist, and you must have some leg movement."

She stormed off, taking my hope of ever walking again with her.

For the next few days, I sank deeper into despair, pleading with nurses and other therapists to help me. They told me that it was up to Beth. Sensing my emotional state, my father and younger brother, Steve, flew from the East Coast to see me in the hospital. While it was great to see them, every time I

looked at my father, I saw how deeply he was hurting. One
day while Wanice and my dad were visiting, I was struggling
through physical therapy, trying to scoot across a mat. I
glanced over at Dad. He was watching me with the most
painful look on his face. He sensed my frustration at having
trouble trying to perform a task a two-year-old could perform
better. A tear ran down his cheek. I'm sure he was remembering the days I was on the track team and had outrun everyone
at a school of over two thousand students. Suddenly, my
thoughts went back many years, to an event that took place
between my father and me when I was sixteen.

"Dad, I'm going to beat you this time," I said with a glow-
ing excitement in my voice.

"We'll see, Son, but I wouldn't count your victory quite yet.
I've still got some kick left."

We walked up to the end of the road that ran in front of our
house.

Turning around and facing back in the direction from which
we had come, we both knew the moment had arrived.
Stretching before us was a one-hundred-yard-long marked
track, the end being our driveway.

"Dad, when this is over you are going to be eating my dust,"
I exclaimed with boyhood bravado.

"Yeah, okay, champ, let's see who is going to be eating
whose dust. You've never beaten me yet. I know the day is
coming, but not today," he said chuckling.

"Dad, how did you get to be so fast?"

"When I was young, I was the fastest kid in my neighbor-
hood. But when I was twelve years old, a truck ran over my
left leg and broke it just above the knee. The doctors reset my
leg, and we prayed for the best. Soon, I could walk with the

cast on, but it was so painful that I used to bite down on a stick to keep from crying out. In a few months, they took the cast off and I began jogging slowly despite the pain. Within another few months, I was actually faster than I was before I broke my leg. I eventually became one of the fastest kids in the state of South Carolina. I had a dream to run again and I didn't let anybody stop me."

I idolized my dad, but I knew the outcome of the race that day was going to go my way. The little boy in me didn't want to beat him. However, the man in me wanted him to eat my dust.

"Dad, you say 'Go.' I don't want you to have any excuses when this is over."

"Okay, Son. On your mark, get set. . . ."

It seemed like an eternity waiting for him to say "Go." My dad was in great shape for a forty-year-old. He had beaten me every time, but I was ready for him. Every muscle in my body was ready. My adrenaline raced, my young heart pumped blood to my pulsating muscles. I knew without a doubt this was the day.

"Go!"

We shot out of our still positions like bullets out of a gun. We were dead even after several yards. I ran like the wind with every muscle performing with 100 percent efficiency. At fifty yards we were still dead even. I had never been able to stay with him this long before! After seventy-five yards we were still even, but I sensed he was tiring. I knew he wasn't a quitter, and I was going to have to outwork him. My body gave me an additional surge of energy, and I started pulling away. As we crossed the finish line I was ahead by two full strides.

"I did it!" I yelled at the top of my lungs. I regained my breath as we both slowed down. I glanced back to Dad only to see a strange look on his face. Two conflicting emotions were being portrayed on his face. One was happiness; the other was sadness. This seemed very strange to me.

"What's wrong, Dad?" I asked as we stopped running and I walked back to him.

"Son, the only way you will understand how I feel right now is to go through it yourself," he said, still trying to catch his breath.

"Two things are going through my mind. I am so proud of you. I have always told you the day you could outrun me you would be a man. Of course, I was joking, but as I look at you, I see you are a man. I know you have worked very hard for this moment. The other thing I am thinking is that I am growing old. That's something you won't experience for awhile, but I know that someday your son will do it to you. You'll see. It will be one of the happiest and saddest days of your life." He paused for a moment still breathing heavily.

"But I can still out–arm wrestle you," he said, hitting me on the shoulder and laughing. We walked back to the house slowly, and I thought about what he had told me.

The Race Begins

The memory faded. I was still staring at Dad. Sitting right next to Dad watching my therapy was my son. Suddenly I realized, for the first time, I would never have the same experience with my sons. I would never race them, chase them or even walk with them. The thought of this tremendous loss hit me square between the eyes. Now the tears flowed down my cheeks. I lay down on the mat, hoping if I didn't look at them anymore, I could ignore the feelings that were racing through my mind. It didn't work. I found myself crying out loud. I was embarrassed to be crying in front of my father and all of the other patients, but I couldn't stop.

After finishing my therapy session that day, I tried to talk with my family. I tried to explain to Dad what had happened, but it was difficult to tell him how I felt without having him worry about me. I just told him I was having a bad day, and we both dropped it. But as I watched Dad walk away, I remembered he, too, faced a similar battle and won.

Then I heard a little voice in my heart: *Rob, run the race.*

"Run the race"? I can't even stand up, much less run a race.

Rob, you have everything you need to run the race, an inner voice answered.

I was not sure what the voice meant, but I knew I had to try. Dad had done it; now it was my turn. I knew I would never run a foot race with my children, much less win one, but I could run the race of life in such a way that I could win other races. I could also encourage my sons by example to run their own races.

Now I was more determined than ever. I talked with the hospital chaplain about my problems with Beth and finally decided to talk to her supervisor. Beth's supervisor was understanding but surprised that Beth hadn't been more supportive. She told me that Beth was one of their best therapists and assured me that my therapy would move forward.

The next day I asked Beth once again about the possibility of walking with braces and crutches. This time, her answer was different.

"This is a big waste of time, but here is a list of *all* of the things you must do in order to walk with braces and crutches," she said.

"Thank you, Beth. I promise that I'll work hard, and whatever is on this list, I'll give it my best try," I said. But she just walked off, muttering something under her breath.

I looked at the list. *Maybe Beth is right. Maybe it is impossible!* The list was staggering, filled with requirements that consisted of strength, endurance, increased range of motion on my legs and much more. That night after my workday was over, I lay in bed reading the list of requirements, trying not to feel overwhelmed at the task that lay before me. In order to meet all of the requirements, I would have to be able to stretch both of my legs to a 120-degree angle lying on my back. I would have to pass a rigorous cardiovascular and oxygen test, which entailed pushing bike pedals with my hands, for as long as I could. Then there was a minimum time on the endurance track that I had to meet, while still keeping my heart rate down at a tolerable level. In addition, there were many other agility exercises. I would have to be able to do fifty parallel bar dips without stopping, then stand up for one hour at a standing table. Next I had to balance myself in the twenty-five-foot-long parallel bars using braces. I had to "walk" (swinging my legs) not less than two times the length of the bars. After reading the list, I was almost numb at the thought of this awesome undertaking. I was a weight lifter before my accident, so I was fairly confident that I could work up to and do *some* of the tasks on the daunting list. But the killer was the very last item, number eighteen: leg movement. All the hard work and determination in the world will not rejuvenate severed nerves. This was going to have to be God's territory. I was glad that I was

finally going to be given a chance, though, and was determined to try my best—in spite of what the therapist said.

Beth's voice kept echoing in my mind: "I know that we
would just be wasting my time. You must have some leg
movement in order to walk."

I thought about the helplessness of my situation. I wanted
to walk, yet realistically, it was impossible without leg movement. I thought about how much easier it would be just to forget the whole thing. But I couldn't. I believed with all of my
heart that I was going to walk again. I was determined that I
was going to do everything I could to accomplish my dreams.
I would leave the rest in God's capable hands.

Fighting Back

The very next morning, I started working even harder than
I ever had before. My hamstring muscles were currently being
stretched to 90 degrees. I asked one of the therapists to stretch
my legs at least three degrees further each day, so that ten days
later both of my legs would be at the required 120. With the
aid and encouragement of this therapist, and spurred on by the
desire to walk again, I made it in only eight days.

In my weight-lifting class I worked like a horse. There were
two sets of pulley systems that were used to work on the
muscles necessary to walk using braces and crutches. One was
the "lat pull" and it exercised the latissimus (back) muscles. It
consisted of a bar over the head that was pulled down to the
chest and then behind the head. The other was a bar that was
chest-high, which had to be pushed down as far as the legs to

work the triceps. I took a good, hard look at both pulley systems before explaining my goals to the weight-lifting director.

"Bill, I want to try to walk again and Beth tells me that I need to be stronger. What is the current record for a combined pull using both of the pulley systems?"

"The standing record is 285 pounds set a few years ago by a former weight lifter."

"What is the maximum lift that you feel would be safe for me to attain?"

"The maximum weight that we are allowed to put on the weight system is 300 pounds, 150 pounds for each of the two exercises. That is a great deal of weight to pull in the sitting position and with your level of injury. You can't just jerk it down, you have to power it down. Besides, jerking this kind of weight is dangerous with your back injury."

Naturally, I decided that my goal would be the maximum, 300 pounds, and setting a new record was just an added plus, I figured.

I began with 100 pounds, and increased this weight by five pounds each day. Two weeks later, in a routine weight class, Bill set up the first pulley system for 150 pounds. The other patients were looking on in disbelief, but I believed I could do it. He tightened the wheelchair seatbelt because that much weight could actually lift me right out of the chair. I took a few deep breaths, said a silent prayer, then looked at Bill and said, "Here goes!"

Directly over my head was a bar that was attached to a cable. The cable was fed through a pulley system to weights that were placed behind me. I had to pull the bar down to my chest to lift the weights. Bill positioned himself next to me as a spotter in case I got into trouble. Slowly, I started to pull, but the weights didn't move. So I pulled harder. The weights began lifting off of the ground. I continued to pull down even though my back was beginning to hurt. Nothing was going to stop me. I pulled the bar down below my chin and even with my chest. I had done it! As a matter of fact, I did it three more times!

"Set me up on the second event, Bill," I said as the onlooking patients cheered.

I could feel my heart pumping adrenaline to my muscles as I waited for Bill to set up the second and much more difficult lift.

"Okay, it's all up to you," Bill said with a supportive voice.

I placed my hands on the bar that was now chest-high in front of me. I now had to put my hands on the bar and push it down to my lap. This exercise used triceps almost exclusively. I began driving the bar down slowly. I pushed the bar all the way down to my legs. This time, the weights moved even more easily and smoothly than before, so I pumped out five more pulls. Another round of applause went up around me. Bill just stood there with a proud look on his face and declared, "Rob, you are going to walk out of this hospital."

Soon after, I went to the parallel bars for the big day: fifty parallel bar dips. I had done forty-five the day before, and I knew this was it. So did Bill! He even told other therapists that I was going to make it that day, so several of them gathered around to watch me, too. I began counting, "One, two, three . . ." I fell into a comfortable rhythm while lifting myself up and down. Soon I was up to twenty-five, then thirty, then thirty-five. When I reached forty-five, the therapists began to count with me out loud.

I was totally exhausted as we all counted out the last three together, ". . . forty-eight, forty-nine, fifty!"

They erupted into applause, but behind their eyes I thought I saw sadness. I knew what it was. They knew that even with all my hard work, I could not rejuvenate nerves and that the required leg movement was not going to happen.

One by one, I whittled away at the requirements on my list. And each morning I would again try to lift my legs, hoping for that miracle. Each time I rolled away disappointed, but not discouraged. I still had more work to do. The standing table was the next challenge. I stood at the table for increasingly longer times until at last I could stand for one hour, using straps to hold the bulk of my weight. Soon I could actually stand at the table without straps for an hour at a time. Then I actually "walked" between the parallel bars using two temporary, long leg braces that reached from my upper thighs and attached to shoes. They locked at the knee and were strapped on with straps and buckles. They were very heavy and cumbersome, but Beth's goal for me was to walk to the end and back two times. I did it twenty times! It was so exciting to almost feel as if I were walking again, even though my hands and arms were doing all the work. I only quit because the time was up, not because I was tired.

Finally, I had checked off everything on the eighteen-point list except for leg movement. But, since this was in God's hands and beyond my control, I just continued working and praying for a miracle. "Those of steadfast mind you keep in peace—because they trust in you," it says in Judah's Song of Victory, in Isaiah 26:3. I believed and trusted.

Who Moved That Leg?

On the morning of March 24, with about three weeks to go before my release, a strange thing happened. I finished dressing but had to wait for help to put on my shoes. My legs were still very heavy from my days as a weight lifter so I asked a nurse to give me a hand. She was struggling to lift my leg when I instinctively tried to raise my leg so that she could put my left shoe on. My leg raised up off of the bed about an inch and then crashed back down. She looked at me and I looked at her—I thought she had done it and she thought I had done it.

"Do that again!" she half-screamed with a crazy look in her eyes.

"Do what again? I can't lift my legs."

"Rob, I've got news for you; I can't lift your legs either! Do it again!"

"I'll try," I said, amazed. This time I lifted it up about four inches before it slowly descended to the bed.

"Don't go away," she said, running out into the hall like a wild woman. She returned with a dozen excited nurses, therapists, aides and doctors.

"I understand you just did something out of the ordinary," my doctor said with a skeptical look on his face. He heard that hands were under my legs the first time my leg lifted.

The doctor had the list—the one that I had been working so hard on—in his hands. His pen was poised above the very last item, number eighteen: leg movement. So much depended on the next few seconds. I took a deep breath and said a quick prayer.

"Just watch this," I said, willing every bit of energy I had into my numb leg. This time it rose more than a foot above the bed. I even held it there for about three seconds before it fell back on the bed. By this time, my roommates were trying to see through the crowd that surrounded me. Everyone was amazed at what had just happened. While some shook their heads in disbelief, others cheered. The doctor checked off the last item on the list and wrote a few notes. Then, while most of the others went back to whatever they had been doing, he stood there for a long time, lost in deep thought. I think he knew he had just witnessed a miracle. Some of my roommates were encouraged by what they had seen, and thought if they worked harder, too, anything was possible. I believed that to be true, but I also explained that I attributed the miracle to prayer first and hard work second.

Two days later the big event came. I was going to walk outside of the parallel bars for the first time. At the appointed time I went into the physical therapy room and began the long, tedious task of putting my braces on, which I had been doing for over a week. This took about half an hour of frustration and hard work. With little movement in my left leg and no movement in my right leg, it was a nearly impossible task. But I finally finished and stood up between the parallel bars to stretch out my back and work on my balance. I was going to need more balance using two crutches than the stable parallel bars I had grown accustomed to. One of the therapists walked over with a smile on her face and said, "Let's do it."

I rolled, and they walked into the hall. George, the largest male therapist, was there to help in case I started to fall. I was still uneasy, because I probably outweighed him, too, but I was glad he was there, just in case. Mary, the head therapist, explained how I was to use the crutches to push off with, and then by moving them to the front quickly, I could stop the forward movement before falling. She also explained that because I could not functionally move my legs, I would use gravity to move them forward. In other words, by putting the crutches in front of me, at the approximate width of my shoulders, my legs would hop up to the crutches using them for support and balance. This gait was called a "swing-to," because you swing your legs forward to meet the crutches.

"Are you ready, Rob?" Mary asked, still smiling.

"Yes, I'm a little scared, but I've come too far to turn back now."

"Good! You may get up whenever you like then. I have confidence you will do fine."

Here it was. For three months I had worked for and anticipated this moment. I was trying to concentrate solely on this one important event, but it was difficult with Beth standing right by me with her usual bitter expression. I wished that she could have been the one who was encouraging me and sharing the excitement with me. But I tried not to dwell on the past and tried concentrating on the event that was before me.

"Here goes," I said, pushing on my crutches. Everyone moved into position in order to support me. Because I wasn't sure how hard to push, I had underestimated my weight and did not fully stand up. I crashed back down to the waiting wheelchair. The second time, putting more arm strength into it, I flew up to the standing position and was falling over forward when I caught myself with my crutches.

"I'm up!" I cried, not believing I was actually standing up.

"Very good, but let's try standing up a few more times so that you get the hang of it," Mary said in an encouraging tone.

"Anything you say—this is a great feeling," I said, beaming.

I carefully sat down with Mary's instruction as to how far to be away from the chair. With two straight leg braces, once I started down, I was going and I couldn't change direction or distance relative to the chair. After I made several attempts at standing, Mary said the words I had been waiting to hear for months.

"Let's go for a walk!"

"I'm ready," I said, getting in position to take my very first step as a paraplegic. I knew somewhere, thousands of miles away, that Granny was praying. I could feel her love and prayers. A tear ran down my cheek as I realized the significance of the moment. George turned his head so I couldn't see his tears. He later told me that he had never seen anyone walk with my level of injuries.

I planted my crutches up ahead and got ready for the hop. I wasn't sure how hard to push so I pushed down on my arms and tried to hop. My body swung forward on my arms and I almost went over forward, but I caught myself. I forgot that I did not have any rear muscles with which to keep myself from falling over forward. Trying to compensate for this inequity, I learned that I must always keep the crutches well out in front of me. The effort was enormous, and I was glad that I had worked as hard as I did to get to this place; I needed all the stamina and endurance I could get. I took another eleven steps before I was exhausted. I sat back down in my chair and rested.

"That was very good for your first attempt. I think we should go ahead with ambulating trials, Rob. Many people cannot even take one step their first time outside of the parallel bars," Mary said as Beth walked away without saying a word.

During the last two weeks of my stay at Rancho, I spent my time walking in the parallel bars for several hours and taking at least one walk a day outside of the bars. Beth worked with me on improving my stance and gait. We also worked on

falling and standing back up. It would be several months
before I would have confidence in falling correctly and getting
back up. My longest walk while still in the hospital was
approximately fifty feet.

While I was learning to walk again, Wanice was bravely
facing the responsibilities of raising our two children and
making all of the arrangements for our move back to Texas.
We decided we needed all the help from family we could get
at this time, and I couldn't go back to working on oil rigs
anyway.

To understand how hard she had it, you have to visualize this
timetable: I had left Wanice and our son in Texas to start my
new job in California in July. Then she and Jason had moved
away from all our family and friends in Texas to join me in
California in September. We joined a church in October and the
accident happened in November. Our second son was born a
month later. All this time she was pregnant and then had a newborn and a two-and-a-half-year-old to care for, plus trying to
visit me two and a half hours away several times a week.

"It was definitely a 'God-thing,'" Wanice recalls of that
awful time, and referring to our church friends the Wilsons
and the Petersons, who virtually adopted us though they
barely knew us. "They just decided to be there for us, no
matter what." Thank God for them, because we didn't have
time to get to know any of the families of the people I worked
with those few months. They were practically all we had in
terms of family or friends in California. Although it's a blur
now, Wanice remembers how "really busy" I was at rehab during the day, "always working on something," while she tried
to arrange one day a week to visit by herself, one day with
both babies and maybe one day with just one of the boys. The

Wilsons and the Petersons helped her tremendously with meals, taking turns with the boys, and sometimes accompanying her to the rehab hospital to watch the boys so she could visit with me for a little while. All of this was so hard on us as a young couple with two babies, being separated and facing such an uncertain future. Even finding a place to talk together privately was hard to come by at the hospital. But Wanice also gratefully remembers "never a bit of car trouble" to contend with, "not even a flat tire" in all those miles over crowded freeways and through notorious L.A. traffic. She and I both know that, as busy as God was answering my prayers for leg movement, he was also riding with her, keeping the engine running smoothly and soothing the antsy little ones in the backseat during the long, grueling drive each way.

Chapter 3

Two Steps Forward and One Step Back

*Whether you think you can, or think you can't,
you're right.*

—*Thomas Alva Edison*

Homecoming

In preparation for my eventual homecoming, I went home for two weekends a month to slowly reintroduce me to the environment. April was my first trip.

While I was happy to be home, it was blatantly obvious that I was now "handicapped." In the hospital I was like everyone else around me, and the strongest on the ward. At home, I felt weak and awkward as my wheelchair bumped into walls and prevented me from going certain places. It was difficult explaining to Jason that I couldn't do everything I used to do, but he seemed to understand, as much as a three-year-old could. He'd look at me as if I was a stranger, and say, "I can't wait until you're better and can walk again," as if I had a cold.

Wanice was very emotional and would go from laughing hysterically to sobbing without reason. My first night home I needed a bath. Since we couldn't get my wheelchair to the upstairs bathroom, she had the ingenious idea to spray me outside with a garden hose. I took off my clothes and went out to the porch, which was surrounded by a low wall. She sprayed me and I shivered as the cold water hit me full-force. As I wiped the soap from my eyes, I looked up and noticed that any one of our twenty neighbors could see me in all my glory from the apartments above. We burst out laughing and continued giggling until I was dry. When we returned to the house, she burst out crying. She couldn't tell me why. I realized she had probably been crying every day since I was away. I put my own emotions aside, and began trying to meet her emotional needs.

The next day I called my boss. It was important to me that he knew I wasn't bitter toward him or the company about what happened. I was also anxious to return to work, although I had a dreaded feeling that there might not be a job for me to return to. He invited Wanice and I to dinner.

After church the next day, Wanice and I went to Jim and Mary's house. As I watched Jim flip the steaks on the grill, he brought me up to date on the goings-on at work. After a few awkward moments of silence I said: "Jim, we both know that the oil field is no place for a paraplegic. I was wondering if you could use an extra salesperson."

He didn't say anything for what seemed like an eternity. After a long pause he lowered his eyes to the ground as he spoke. "Rob, I'm sorry to say that we're not busy enough to need a salesperson. It hurts me to say this, but I don't think we can use your services any longer." He added, "But I did talk to your old boss who said that he might be able to use you at the corporate office in Fort Worth."

Jim's face looked wracked with guilt. I tried to make a joke about fitting a wheelchair in the corporate washrooms, and then changed the subject.

The next week I called Jim Robertson at the corporate office.

He regretfully told me that they were in the middle of a hiring freeze and that they had no money to hire anyone at the moment. He advised me to stay in touch.

With that, another part of me was crushed. How was I going to support my family? Our medical bills were mounting, our savings was running out, and now I was without a paycheck. That night in my prayers, I turned my situation over to God.

✻ ✻ ✻

The next week, I called Jim back.

"Rob, I'm so glad you called," he said. "I spoke with the president of the company, and he told me there's a position here for you. We can definitely use you back here. Since you left to go out in the field, our technical writing program has fallen by the wayside. When can you start?"

I hung up the phone elated, thanking God for answering my prayers. Once again, things were looking up. I was home with my family, I had a job again, and if therapy continued, I would be walking on my own.

In June, I became an outpatient at the Dallas Rehabilitation Institute for continued therapy. One day, while leaving the hospital, I felt something pop in my back. While I assumed I had just pushed myself during therapy, I thought it best to check it out. The X rays revealed bad news.

"The pain you feel is caused by one of the steel rods that were placed in your back during surgery," the doctor said. "It has completely popped out of line. The rods will need to come out. If your backbone has not fused properly, I will need to replace them. If the backbone has fused, I'll simply remove the rods."

I asked him just how "simple" it would be.

"If we just remove the rods, your stay will be three weeks. If I replace them, you'll need to be hospitalized for six weeks."

"Six weeks!" *Two steps forward, three steps back.*

Yet Another Operation

Once again, I could view life from two different perspectives. I could feel sorry for myself or I could concentrate on what was really important—my health. I decided to focus on the solution rather than self-pity. If surgery was my solution, I would get through it as best as I could. We scheduled the operation and it went smoothly, yet I awoke to considerable pain.

"Rob," came a familiar voice from the darkness, "Are you okay?"

I became aware that my eyes were closed. Upon opening them, I was looking Wanice square between the eyes.

"How do you feel?" she asked with concern in her face.

"My back is killing me. Please get me a painkiller right away."

She quickly disappeared into the hall to get a nurse. While I was waiting I noticed a funny thing. The ceiling was moving. *The ceiling was moving?* That didn't make sense. I shook my head thinking that the drugs were causing me to hallucinate. When I saw a vase in the corner, I noticed that it was moving, too. *What was going on?* I realized that the objects were not moving, *I* was. The bed was slowly tilting to the side. Within seconds I was facing the wall. I had a sudden flash of terror as I wondered, *Was I going to fall out?* Then I realized my arms and legs were strapped down to the bed. I was going to fall and I couldn't do anything about it. But just as soon as I was going to call for help, it stopped tilting and headed back the other way. The bed continued until I had tilted 180 degrees and was facing the other wall. Then it stopped once again, and I headed back in the opposite direction. When I found myself staring back at the door, Wanice and a nurse reentered. The nurse gave me a shot in my arm and told me that I could have one every four hours. I didn't know how I was going to survive four hours between shots, but I shook my head to acknowledge her statement. The nurse left and I looked back at Wanice. I could tell by the grim look on her face what the doctor had had to do, but I asked anyway.

"What did Dr. Wharton do to my back?"

"He had to replace the Herrington Rods [seventeen-inch steel rods] in your back and re-fuse your backbone with a piece of your iliac crest from your hip bone. He said you are going to have to wear a body jacket for six months," she said with a look of compassion.

"Six months? What is this contraption I'm laying on anyway? I feel seasick on this machine."

"It's a Stryker frame. It is designed to rotate your body and keep the weight off your back most of the time. Sorry, Honey, they said you will be on it for over a week."

A week? Could I survive having my arms and legs tied down, rotating twenty-four hours a day for seven days? What choice did I have? I'd have to be tougher than the circumstances. I soon realized that, as uncomfortable as it was, it did work. The pain lessened to a bearable amount, but the boredom was really tough. I couldn't watch TV because half of the time I was facing the walls and I couldn't see the screen. I couldn't read a book because my arms were strapped down and I couldn't hold it. My friends started coming by, but I wasn't very much company as it was even painful to talk. Yet, the days crept by, and on the eighth day, my body jacket was delivered, and I was placed into a standard bed along with the jacket I would wear for the next six months. On the tenth day, I was moved to Dallas Rehabilitation Institute for at least three weeks of therapy and recovery.

For the first couple of days, I had to remain in bed because a nasty staph infection attacked the incision on my back. At first, I had to relearn how to live, dress, bathe, work, and play in a body jacket. I had forgotten just how painful and confining it was. I couldn't reach anything or lean forward without the body jacket cutting into my legs. I couldn't exercise very much at all without my back hurting or my body jacket getting in the way.

Like most tragedies, the full impact didn't hit me at first. Then one night, with about twenty of my friends at my bedside, it finally caught up with me. I watched with envy and anger as my friends walked around my bed with strong legs. When they innocently chatted about playing tennis together at a later date, I broke down. Suddenly, anger gave way to sorrow and self-pity, and I began to cry out loud. "I'm so tired of it," I sputtered. "I'm tired of the pain and handicaps. I want to be normal and play a game of tennis with you guys. I want to be strong again!" I was so embarrassed. Several of them just put their arms around me or held my hand while I wept. Everyone grew quiet. They all felt as helpless as I did.

The Burns

Two weeks later, I went home a defeated man. I returned to work after another two weeks, but my spirit was crushed, and I was not happy or productive. For the next three months, a home nurse came by each night to help me dress. She cleaned my incision (still painfully infected), and helped with baths and hygiene. I didn't like my privacy being invaded, but it was either this or stay in the hospital. I needed the nurse to help me with my daily routines. She started the water running in my baths and helped me out of my clothes. She transferred me from the bed to the wheelchair and from the wheelchair to a bath seat (only my legs were in the water). I was looking forward to the day when I could take a real bath without my body jacket so I could really get clean.

One night during my bath I saw steam rising out of the tub. Looking over, I noticed the mirror was covered with steam. Peering down at the water that was streaming across my feet, I noticed red spots on the top part of my feet. I reached down to turn on some more cold water and realized it wasn't on at all! The nurse had forgotten to turn on the cold water. With no sensation from the waist down, I had no way of feeling if the water was hot or cold. I pulled myself out of the tub as quickly as I could and looked down at my feet and calves. They were severely blistered. I called the nurse and she came in and readjusted the water—as if that was going to fix everything! The following morning my feet were so swollen that I couldn't even put on shoes. I went to the hospital, where I learned I had second-degree burns halfway up my calves. The doctor told me that I couldn't put pressure on the burns by walking for at least two months. *Another step forward, another step back.*

The Daddy Book

A few days later, Jason told me he wished I were like the dad in one of his books.

"What do you mean, Son? What book?"

"The Daddy Book!"

"Can you get it for me, Jason?" I asked curiously.

He disappeared into his room and returned a few seconds later with *The Daddy Book* in hand. My heart sank as I looked at the illustration on the first page of the book—a father carrying his son high on his shoulders. Each page had a picture of a big, strong daddy playing with his adoring son: They were chasing each other, playing tag, riding bikes together and climbing trees. It was painfully obvious to me just how much Jason wanted me to be like that perfect father pictured on the pages of his book. But what bothered me the most was the look I saw in my son's eyes. It was utter disappointment.

"Jason, I'm sorry I can't be like this dad, but I'll try very hard to do everything I can with you. I want to do all the things in this book, too, but I can't. I hope you can understand that," I told him, trying not to let my own disappointment and hurt show through.

"It's not that I don't want to play with you this way, Son, but it's just not physically possible for me. Do you understand what I mean?"

"Yes, I understand, Dad, but I still cry for you and me because you can't walk."

That was my breaking point. If I wasn't beaten before, I was then. I felt totally defeated. I had open sores on my feet caused by the burns, which kept me from walking with braces and crutches. Jason had doubts that I loved him because I wasn't like storybook dads, or even like his friends' fathers. I was still wrapped up in that painful body jacket from the back surgery—surgery I'd had to have because the first surgeon didn't do a good enough job on me after the accident.

I lay down in my bed and tried to tell Wanice how I felt, but I didn't want to worry her. I was beaten, tired and really didn't care if I lived or died. I went to work Monday through Friday, and went to church on Sunday. Going through the motions of day-to-day life, I was able to fool most people into thinking I was happy, but I knew better.

Several weeks after *The Daddy Book* conversation, I found myself once again playing with Jason outside. We were launching water rockets.

"Really fill it up this time, Dad!" Jason said with a look of excitement on his face.

I filled a little red plastic rocket to the halfway mark and placed it onto a hand-held rocket pump. It was a pneumatic rocket that worked by pumping air into the half water-filled body. Once the pressure was released, the rocket shot upward. Pumping the handle about ten times, I held the rocket out in front of me and released the holding mechanism. The rocket spewed water and air all over me, sending the rocket flying fifty feet into the air. Jason screamed with delight and ran over to our driveway and retrieved the rocket for the third time. Our front yard was big enough to handle the trajectory if the rocket went straight up and down, which is what it had done on every launching attempt thus far.

"Come on, Dad, really pump it hard this time. I want to see it disappear into the clouds."

This time I pumped on the handle about twenty-five times. Water was spewing from the pressure chamber so I repeated the launching procedure. All of a sudden, a gust of wind blew by at the precise moment I launched the rocket and carried the rocket over the front yard and beyond the house. Jason and I went into the backyard to look for the rocket but it became clear that the wind had carried it even farther, over the back-yard fence. It was gone.

"Let's go get it, Dad."

"Son, I can't. I can't climb over the fence in my wheelchair."

There was no way to retrieve it without going into the rough field that lay behind the fence. Not only did we not even have a gate opening into the field, it had rained recently, so the field would be a muddy mess. My wheelchair would get stuck. And even if I could get to the field and try to walk through the mud, high grass and potholes with my braces, I would have to walk well over three hundred yards to get to the wayward rocket. Even if I was game, my previous "walking" record was less than one hundred feet, and that was before my recent back surgery. Nope, we wouldn't be seeing that rocket again.

Jason acted like it didn't matter and began playing with something else. I sat there thinking of all of the possible ways to retrieve the rocket, but they all seemed unreasonable to fetch a rocket that was only worth two dollars. I went back into the house, but the rocket haunted me. The next day at work, I couldn't concentrate on anything because of that stupid rocket. After several days, my feelings of frustration had only grown worse.

Then, almost a week later, I was in the backyard pushing

Jason on the swings. No matter which way I faced, I couldn't ignore that fence. It seemed to me a constant reminder of my handicap. I turned to go back into the house. I was halfway to the door when I stopped and just lost it. I couldn't stand it anymore. I began beating my wheelchair with my fists.

"Dad, what's wrong?" Jason asked, running over to me with an innocent but worried look on his face. I turned around and faced the fence that was causing my frustrations.

"It's that rocket, Son. I want to go get it, but I can't. I just can't walk that far."

"Yes, you can, Dad. You can do anything," he said with stars in his eyes as if I was Superman, the Incredible Hulk and He-Man all rolled into one. I knew the most important thing in the world right at that moment was to keep those stars in his eyes. I didn't ever want to see the look of disappointment I had seen in them the day we looked through *The Daddy Book* together. I knew he understood there were some things I couldn't do, but to quit before trying would be a terrible example for both of my sons.

"You know what, Jason? You're right. I *can.*"

We went into the house, and I put my braces on. I didn't know how I was going to retrieve that rocket, but I knew I was going to try. I rolled past the front yard and down the block in my chair with Jason singing battle songs as if we were going to fight a war. Ten minutes later, I reached the edge of the field, and began pushing my chair through the high grass and mud. I'd barely gone twenty feet when my wheelchair became firmly stuck. I had no choice. I grabbed my crutches from the back of the wheelchair and began to walk very slowly through the grass and mud. After fifty yards, I was exhausted. I rested for awhile and started again. I knew if I fell so soon after my recent surgery, I could be in real trouble, so I refused to think about it. Now more than halfway there, I struggled on with frequent rest stops. Jason walked ahead and began to play on top of a huge pile of freshly moved dirt. In the midst of all my efforts, I was not paying very close attention to him, or I would have noticed the origin of the pile. Suddenly he screamed and ran back to me. He was covered with biting, stinging fire ants! I tried to brush them off, but I was so unstable leaning on the crutches, I couldn't really reach anything other than Jason's head.

I screamed several times toward our backyard—more than fifty yards away—hoping Wanice would hear me. Finally, her pretty head popped over the backyard fence to see what I was yelling about. She jumped the fence, raced over and brushed most of the ants off of Jason. I watched as they disappeared for home and a change of clothes. I kept on going. No matter what happened, I was going to get that rocket. Soon I came to a grade too steep for me to walk up. I fell forward on the ground and slowly began pulling myself up the embankment on my face. Dragging my crutches behind me, I crept until I came to an ant bed. Now what? My only hope was to get up on my knees and try to crawl like a baby over the anthill. I tried pushing myself up to my knees. Somehow, I did it! I began crawling like my one-year-old. I was really doing it! I hadn't even known I could crawl. From that day on, the boys rode around the house on my back like a horse. This became one of my answers to that superdad in *The Daddy Book*.

I slowly made my way over to our fence and used it to stand up again. I brushed some of the dirt, grass and ants off, then began walking again—ignoring all previous limitations and logical strength barriers. As I approached the area where the rocket should have been, I kept looking, but I couldn't see it because of the tall grass. But you know what? By then, it didn't matter whether I found the plastic rocket or not. The only thing that mattered is that I tried to find it. I walked and crawled slowly back to my wheelchair on the other side of the field. It took me over an hour! I rolled back home satisfied with the knowledge I hadn't let Jason down because I had tried, and I had just walked more than six times farther than my previous record.

Soon after, I bought Jason a new rocket. But all he remembered was the day he and his dad walked through the field together. The stars stayed in his eyes, and I was determined to keep them there. That's when I realized that my self-pity was not only affecting me, it was affecting my whole family. This realization snapped me out of my cycle of self-pity.

I was so intent on being a good role model for my family, I began walking farther and farther. Within six months, I was walking a mile, then two. Then, in a proud or maybe arrogant attempt to choose a challenge my children would always remember, I set a totally unrealistic goal. I decided I was going to walk from Fort Worth to the next big neighboring city—Dallas—a distance of over twenty-four miles. Now, in addition to working and spending time with my family, I began training.

Chapter 4

Leaning
On Faith

We know that all things work together for good for those who love God, who are called according to His purpose.

—Romans 8:28

In Training

On Christmas Day, 1983, I received the best present ever: The plaster body cast I had been confined in for six long months was finally removed. Not wearing it felt wonderful! I was free to move again. I got down on the floor with the kids and played with their new toys. They loved having me on the floor with them, and I crawled around as they jumped on top of me. They enjoyed having a dad who could do so much more with them. They just kept hugging and kissing me. I promised Wanice that I wouldn't put too much strain on my back until I was accustomed to having the body jacket off. I kept my promise. Even though I was anxious to start training for the walk, I didn't start lifting weights until the holidays were over.

My longest walk had been two miles at this point. I was concerned about my progress but I tried not to worry and just trust in God's promise. I was going to have to continue to trust Him. On January 4, 1984, I officially started training for what we named the Miracle Walk that was now exactly six months away. To evaluate my physical progress, I measured my arms and chest. My upper arms were fifteen inches in the flexed position, my chest was forty-four inches around, and my forearms were thirteen inches. My good friend Jim Hurst came over religiously every other day to help me work out. Both he and his wife Jane believed in the Miracle Walk, even though there was little evidence to prove that it was going to be successful. I learned a lot about servanthood through their lives. On the first night, I began lifting 150 pounds on the bench press and was exhausted after only a few repetitions. Jim and I both participated in a game we made up called the bench-press marathon. This is how it worked: If we could lift it more than five times, we increased the weight ten pounds. Then we took off ten pounds on each repetition until we were down to the bar itself. By that time, we had trouble lifting our arms, much less the bar.

I also built a set of parallel bars in my garage with pipes from a hardware store. At first I could only lift myself about twenty times. That was a far cry from the fifty parallel-bar body lifts I had managed to do in the rehabilitation center; I just hadn't been practicing for a long time. I set a goal of fifty lifts. Jim and I started the first of the most serious, muscle-tearing, bone-wrenching, heart-pounding workouts in which we had ever participated. I concentrated on training for the walk in my wheelchair because I found that when I walked too much, the braces caused sores to develop on my feet and legs. I was going to have to develop my strength with weights and increase my endurance with the racing wheelchair. In my eyes, the secret was not to *be able* to walk that far, but to be *strong* enough to walk the distance. While my strength and endurance in walking were going to be theoretically realized, they wouldn't be actually realized until the day of the Miracle Walk. The truth was that my legs and feet couldn't handle that kind of punishment more than once.

Within weeks, I was able to lift 225 pounds on the bench press at least ten times. I was curling a thirty-five pound dumbbell with each arm at least thirty times. (In the sitting position, that wasn't easy.) Jim and I set various goals for ourselves, and we began meeting them one by one. I was up to twelve miles on the chair at a fast speed. I was pushing my chair at a pace of less than five-and-a-half minutes. I would push my chair faster and faster until I thought my heart would stop and my lungs would burst, then I would go a little farther.

Everything was going well with our training program except for my parallel-bar dips. I was stuck in the forty-repetition range, and I could not seem to do any more. The weeks dragged on, and I was getting nowhere. It was so frustrating, but I had set a goal that I felt was realistic and I was not going to give up until I reached it.

The farthest that I had walked was three-and-one-half miles, after which I was thoroughly exhausted. My feet began to break down, so I decided that I was working too much in the braces and not enough on weights and in the chair. It did concern me, though, that my feet and legs began to bleed in such a short distance compared to the goals that lay before me, but I trusted that God would work that out, too.

The California Connection

In March 1984, Wanice and I flew out to California on business. We were met at the airport by Bob and Ruthie Peterson, who drove us straight to Rancho Los Amigos. I wanted to show Beth, my former therapist, my progress. I prayed all the way there that I would be able to talk with her without any bitterness. I especially didn't want to come across as if I were saying, "I told you I could do it." I was so nervous as I walked across the parking lot into the hospital. It was not until then that I realized just how far I had come. It just didn't seem real that I was actually walking back into Rancho. When I left, I had been totally dependent on the chair.

As soon as I walked into my old ward building, I was surrounded by nurses and aides who remembered me, all hugging and kissing me excitedly. They were all shocked beyond words at my progress; however, my real appointment at Rancho was in physical therapy. It was about lunchtime, and I was told that the therapists were outside holding a barbecue for the patients. I saw Beth as soon as I walked outside. She was about thirty feet away with her back to me. I walked about ten steps and then called her.

"Beth!"

I could tell by the way she was slowly turning around that she had recognized my voice. As she pivoted slowly, her eyes popped open.

"Rob? I can't believe it. Look at you walk!"

I walked the rest of the way over to her, and she gave me a big hug. I was surprised but happy that she seemed glad to see me. She asked me several questions about my new braces; she was impressed with how light they appeared to be. As she avoided mention of our past difficulties, I figured she was either attempting to ask for forgiveness, or she was giving an Oscar-winning performance. Beth actually seemed thrilled to see me. It was quite a change from the "control freak" who had discouraged my every hope of walking after the accident. She told me that because she was a fairly new therapist, she mistook my ultra-positive attitude as a challenge of her knowledge and authority. In hindsight, she said, she wished she had more patients like me, who believed in themselves instead of accepting a grim prognosis. I was really glad that our reunion went so well. I told her that I attributed my recovery to prayer and hard work.

As Bob, Ruthie, Wanice and I walked back to the car, I faced another part of my past that caused me to realize how thankful I should be, and to whom I owed all my thanks. We were in the car and getting ready to leave when I saw a familiar person roll by in his wheelchair. It was Mike—a young man who started ambulation trials on the same day as I had. He, according to Beth, had a far greater chance of walking than I did because he was younger and lighter. I was anxious to talk with him about his progress. I asked Bob to stop by the car that Mike was getting into. "Mike! Remember me? It's Rob Bryant."

"Oh, yeah. Hi, Rob, how are you doing?"

"I'm just fine. I'm walking farther and farther. As a matter of fact, I have walked over three miles nonstop. How about you? Are you walking? Are you moving your legs at all?" I asked. I could tell by his reaction that I was saying the wrong thing. Then I looked down at his legs where the answer was obvious. His limbs had atrophied and were virtually skin and bones due to lack of use.

"No, it was too hard. I finally gave up," he said, looking away sadly and maneuvering into his car. I wished that I had never opened my mouth, but there was no way I could take my words back. I wished him luck, said good-bye, and we left for Camarillo. All the way there I thought about Mike and hoped that maybe he would try again now, knowing it was possible with hard work. But the more I thought about it, the more I realized that all of the hard work in the world won't rejuvenate nerves as had happened to me. My healing was pure grace, and I should be ever mindful of from where my blessing had come. There would have been no way for me to take one step without God's help. According to Beth, walking was impossible for me.

Soon we arrived in Camarillo. The whole Pleasant Valley gang threw a homecoming party for us at Jeff and Judy Wilson's house. It was great to see everyone again. Everyone was amazed at the tremendous progress I had made in the past year. Since I wouldn't be able to lift weights during the long weekend, I decided that I was not going to use my wheelchair at all, as a way of staying in training. When Bob and Jeff took me with them to see the beach and the California scenery, I tired quickly, but kept going. I had walked several miles with them before I even realized how far we'd gone.

At church on Sunday, I fulfilled a promise I had made to myself the year before. At the pastor's invitation, I walked down the center aisle and shared my testimony, trusting that the Lord would lead me in what to say. I told the congregation about the great miracles God had accomplished in my life over the past year. Then I finished up with this thought:

"If God in His wisdom allows something precious of yours to be taken away, there is a reason. You may or may not ever learn the reason, but the important aspect of the loss is how we react to the crisis. God promises that no matter what happens, He won't give us any more than we can handle, and if we build our lives on the rock of Jesus, nothing can shake us. We are living in a lost and dying world. When we crumble like sand, the world watches and is reassured that we don't have any answers either. Be thankful for what you have and not bitter for what you have lost. God bless you."

After church, Wanice and I talked with many of the friends we made during our short stay in California the year before. It was wonderful to feel their hugs, and I was thankful for all their good wishes. The next day, we flew home to Texas. I hadn't said anything to anyone, not wanting Wanice or anyone else to worry, I realized that while walking those two days in California, I had developed a bad sore on my right foot. I didn't walk for two weeks after that, hoping it would heal, but it only grew worse with time. Of course, because I couldn't feel it, I had no idea how bad it was.

In April, a friend of mine suggested that I contact some non-profit organizations to see if I could raise money for them during the walk with pledges per mile. I thought that was a great idea—first, because I could help others while fulfilling my own dream, and second, because it would be a way to get publicity for the Miracle Walk, which would really benefit people. I tried a few agencies before phoning the American Paralysis Association, where I spoke with the president, Kent Waltrep. He was very interested and wanted to speak with me. Little did I know how much I would learn from him! He told me all about the research, experimental projects and testing that the APA was funding in an effort to cure paralysis. Then I discovered just what an inspiration Kent Waltrep was to millions of people in the Dallas/Fort Worth area. Until his accident in 1975, Kent was a running back for Texas Christian University in Fort Worth. Though he was left a quadriplegic (paralyzed from the neck down), he never gave up. After a few years of desperately trying to get the latest kind of therapy, he founded the American Paralysis Association. I was so impressed with his fierce determination and winning attitude, we made the decision that I would walk to raise money and awareness for the American Paralysis Association. In May, I began sending out pledge sheets all over the country, from California to New York. The pledges began pouring in and within weeks we had thousands of dollars' worth of pledges for the walk. While I continued the physically grueling task of training for the twenty-four-mile-plus ordeal, now only six weeks ahead, friends took over the fundraising efforts.

Meanwhile, the sore on my foot refused to heal, so I went to the hospital to see my doctor and therapist about it. They were both concerned because they saw right away that it was a decubitus sore (a sore that starts at the bone and works its way out). Dr. Wharton advised me either not to walk as much or, even better, to stay off of it for one month. If I continued walking, Dr. Wharton warned, I could lose my foot.

While I knew he was right, and I respected his medical advice, I couldn't turn back. I decided that I would continue with my plans, but I would find a way to reduce the pressure on the area. That's when I got creative and came up with a foot-saving idea. I asked the orthotics department to put a piece of plastazote (soft rubberized material) around the area of the sore. When I got home, I took a doorknob cutter and cut a hole through my leg brace where the sore was. Then I sanded the plastazote down to a smooth surface that mimicked the contour of my skin. The plastazote prohibited the edge of the circle I had cut out from rubbing against my foot. After I removed the sharp edges of the cut brace with a rasp file, I put the brace back on, and *voila,* a perfect fit. Now I could walk with the sore exposed to the air, which would help heal it, but without pressure on it.

A week before the walk, I went back to the doctor one more time. He couldn't believe the swelling had gone down so

quickly and was convinced that I had stopped walking alto-
gether. Then I showed the brace adjustment to the orthotics spe-
cialist. He, too, was impressed and said that if the adjustment
really worked, he was going to use this technique to help some
of his other patients. He said he'd call it "The Bryant
Technique."

Aside from the obvious problem of my inability to walk
that far on my own, there were only two obstacles left to my
walk. Despite all my efforts, I had yet to complete fifty dips
on the parallel bars. This was more of a mental than a physical challenge because I thought accomplishing this feat was
vital for the confidence I would need to complete the walk. If
I couldn't even finish a preliminary goal, how could I hope to
make it to the finish line? All I could do was keep trying—
there were only fourteen days left. The second obstacle was
getting partners to accompany me along the twenty-four-mile
route. Knowing it would take me three days to walk that far, I
guessed I needed half a dozen friends to walk with me. After
all, they hadn't been training and the intense heat might prove
too much. I didn't feel I could ask any one person to walk
more than a day. As always, God had already worked that one
out in a surprising manner, as I discovered when, with one
week to go, my phone rang.

Guardian Angels

"Hello, Rob. This is Jeff Wilson and Bob Peterson calling
from good ol' Southern California. We were just talking with

our wives, and we want to be there for you on your walk," Jeff said excitedly.

"You guys are too much!" I almost cried. These friends had already been there for Wanice and I in more ways than I could count. "There's no one else I'd rather have walking beside me," I told them.

Perhaps more than anyone, they understood what I had been through in the past eighteen months. And it was their wives who were there when the doctor told me I'd never walk again. It suddenly seemed so right that it would be Jeff and Bob walking alongside me. Although I was convinced I saw the hand of God in all of this, I had to warn them.

"You know guys, it will probably be over 100 degrees here in Texas. Do you think you can handle it?"

"Well, as a matter of fact," Bob answered, "we were really hoping we could come, so we've been working out by running and riding bikes. We'll do whatever you need us to do."

That settled, we figured out the details. They would arrive during the afternoon of June 30. I was so excited I couldn't stand it. It was almost too good to be true! Jim Hurst would walk alongside me as my trainer, and these two close friends would provide moral support, watch traffic and lead me on the safest path.

As I continued to train every day after work, it seemed as if the remaining days were flying by. By now the pledges had surpassed nine thousand dollars. On Friday, June 29, my colleagues at my office wished me well. Many of them prayed with me that I would have victory in a seemingly impossible task.

On Saturday afternoon, Wanice and I drove to the airport to pick up Jeff and Bob. It was so great to see them, and I realized how perfect it was that they were there as we talked strategy and logistics. Jeff was an engineer for the Navy, and he had thought out many of the technical details ahead of time, things such as the placement of the car and using a bike rider to scout ahead. Bob's gift was constant, unwavering encouragement. He never said never. Like the story about the little locomotive who thought he could, Bob convinced me that my Miracle Walk was no mission impossible. I believed even more strongly that with these two winning personalities along for the ride, so to speak, my prospects for victory were good. And I also knew, with the faith that our trio had in God, that wherever my strength failed, I could rely on God to carry me the rest of the way.

Lord, Lift Me Up

It was Saturday, just two days before the walk. Jim and I had one last workout to get through and we both knew what had to be done. I worked out briefly with the dumbbells and on my leg lifts before turning and facing the bull—the parallel bars. As Jim watched me out of the corner of his eye, I rolled the chair over to the bars. Psychologically, I really needed this small victory and we both knew it. The time had come to do it. Without saying a word, Jim walked over to the bars. I knew he was praying for me as he reached down and placed my legs in the strap. I pushed my weight up on top of the bars with my arms and began the dips, up and down, as Jim counted out loud.

"One, two, three, four, five . . . ," he counted as I found a comfortable rhythm. I decided nothing could make me come down off the bars until I heard Jim say that magic number, "Fifty."

"Twenty-one, twenty-two, twenty-three," he counted with a growing excitement in his voice. Although normally at this point I'd be feeling fatigue, I didn't feel tired at all.

"Thirty-one, thirty-two," he continued counting, giving me a knowing look. The muscle tightness began but as my adrenaline began to pump, I kept going.

"Forty-one, forty-two, forty-three," Jim counted, searching my eyes to see how I was doing. A tiny smile crept across his face. I slowed to a crawl, but I refused to admit defeat.

"Forty-five, forty-six, forty-seven," his voice boomed with anticipation. "Forty-eight, forty-nine," he said as I went down for the last one. Every bit of strength I had was gone, and I knew it. This last one would have to come from the heart as I began to push my way up that final time. I almost smiled through the pain when I noticed that Jim was crouching at the knees slightly, then standing up slowly as if to help me push.

"Come on, Rob, you can do it," he yelled, clenching his fists and encouraging me. I kept pushing and somehow found enough strength to get to the top.

"Fifty!" we both screamed together. I fell down into my wheelchair with a thud as we continued to shout with joy. Bob and Jeff entered the garage and celebrated the victory with us as I caught my breath. Then, since my training program was officially complete, we measured my arms. They were a staggering seventeen inches around. They had increased more than two inches in size. My chest was forty-six inches around, having grown more than two inches as well. That last night before the Miracle Walk, I ate enough calories and protein to power up a rocket ship. Wanice fed me every high-energy, low-sugar food she could think of. It looked like Thanksgiving dinner at our dining table. I ate until I thought I would burst, but I knew I was going to need all of the energy I could get.

Everything I could think of was taken care of. I was as ready as I could be for the Miracle Walk. The rest was up to God!

Chapter 5

The
Miracle Walk

A journey of a thousand miles must begin with a single step.

—Lao-tzu

The First Step

Buzzzz. The alarm chimed at 4:25 A.M. Wanice rolled over and turned it off.

"Rob, are you awake?" she asked in a whisper.

"Yes!"

I could hear Bob and Jeff talking quietly in the other room and could tell by their voices that they were just as excited as I was to get going. The night before they had divvied up the chores as to who would grab what gear and pack it. With everything we had to pack in the car—crutches, extra braces, my wheelchair, our snacks, water, first-aid supplies, etc.—careful planning was a must.

Oddly enough, they were such a well-oiled machine you would have thought they'd done this many times before. Part of my job was putting on my braces, checking the rubber padding for my crutch handles and packing two different kinds of gloves. In nervous anticipation, we got the gear together as Wanice was putting oatmeal, toast, cereal and juice on the table. I wasn't hungry considering my excited state, but I knew it was important to be well-nourished for the long day ahead. After breakfast, the three of us climbed into my car and we were off. Within twenty minutes we'd reached the starting point. The Miracle Walk began officially at 6:35 A.M. on July 2.

Considering my longest walk to date had been three-and-a-half miles, I had a long way to go in a very short time. So I

started with a quick pace. I would have to walk eight times farther and maintain as good a time for three straight days as I
had for the three-and-a-half miles. This walk truly was going
to take a miracle, and I knew it. But I trusted that God would
provide one, if this walk was His will, which I believed it was.
The first stopping point was exactly a mile and a half. I
glanced at my watch while resting and saw it was 7:55 A.M.
I was making good time, but had to keep up this pace while I
could. I'd need to finish one third of the walk by nightfall,
since the afternoon sun and fatigue would slow me down to a
snail's pace of one mile an hour, not including breaks. Jeff and
Bob checked my legs for sore places and luckily there were
none. We were off once again.

By 9:00, the temperature was already starting to climb, but
it was cloudy with a slight breeze, so it was bearable. We
weren't sure how I did it, but I walked the next mile and a half
in under one hour. I still was not feeling fatigued. However,
one aspect of the walk I had not anticipated was the tilted
angle of the shoulder of the road. The angle was barely noticeable to a normal walker or rider. But being on crutches, I had
to compensate for it by leaning slightly to the left on each
stride. This began bothering my back and left shoulder. I tried
walking on the opposite shoulder, but this was even worse. So
I crossed the road again and tried to ignore my growing pain
in my back and shoulder. Several times along the way, Jim and
Jay Racz, a student at the University of Texas at Arlington and
a budding photojournalist who'd been following my progress,
joined us. Because Jim had to work all day, he had to leave the
office each time to check on us.

I had walked a torturous six-and-one-half miles by noon
and was really ready when Wanice joined us for lunch at a

pizza place. I stuffed myself on pizza and continued to drink plenty of water to stay hydrated. With the temperature close to one hundred degrees already, the car's air-conditioning felt like blessed relief. But that turned out to be a problem when I tried to get up after lunch. The air-conditioning had caused my hot, sweaty muscles to cramp. The guys helped me outside where I rested in the warm air and tried to loosen my muscles again. I was developing a sore below my knee where a strap was rubbing it. While I continued to rest, Bob and Jeff acted as a racing pit crew—changing my sweaty socks, checking for more sores and rubbing my already-stiff hands. I switched gloves for the first time. The first pair were weight lifting gloves that were soft in the palm area. The second pair were wheelchair gloves, which had a thick rubber pad on the palms. The idea behind changing gloves occasionally was to effectively move the pressure points on my hands around, in an attempt to prevent blisters.

I was on the road again at 1:30 P.M., though I was moving significantly slower. Jeff looked concerned about my pace. After an hour or so, I began hitting a few small hills. They were barely noticeable to a car, but to me on my braces, they were like small mountains. On flat surfaces, I could use my body weight as momentum to fall forward and catch myself with the next leg and crutch, much like an able-bodied person does without crutches. But on the hills, I could not lean any farther than my braced shoes would allow, since I could not bend at the ankles. Each step was a concentrated effort, and I could not use momentum. My stride was much jerkier and required more effort than a smooth gait did.

Meanwhile, the sore below my right knee was growing worse. That's when Jeff got an idea. With typical engineer's logic, he said, "What if we put a knee pad directly on the sore and the strap over that? That way it can't rub you anymore, and it will distribute the pressure exerted by the brace strap."

"That just might work," I replied. As I finished my break, Wanice drove off to buy a knee pad. It worked great! Now at least I didn't have to worry about infections or pressure sores.

By 2:30 P.M., I had walked a total of seven-and-a-half miles, with short stops every mile and a half to rest. This time I took a fifteen-minute break that seemed like five and was off again. Each step was a conscious act of will. I had to keep telling myself, *One more step; each step is one closer to Keist Park.* I was tired and sore everywhere I could feel, but I wasn't giving up. Seeing my energy draining, Bob and Jeff kept encouraging me. Far too much prayer, training and planning had gone into this to give up now.

I came to the foot of a large hill a half hour later and ran out of energy. I simply had nothing left to give. My strength and courage ran out simultaneously, and I knew I was through for the day. The ninety-eight-degree heat had zapped all of the "I-can" attitude out of me. It was 3:30 in the afternoon. I hated to waste daylight, but if I wanted to walk the next day, I was going to have to quit. I felt so disappointed that I had not made my goal of eight-and-one-half miles for the first day. If I expected to complete this walk, I was going to have to make goals and stick to them, but I physically could not walk up one more hill. I had to accept defeat this first day.

By then, Jim and Wanice were there with their cars, so I got into Jim's car and Bob and Jeff climbed in with Wanice. When Jim pulled out of the driveway we were in and out onto the road, I couldn't believe my eyes: There was the eight-and-a-half-mile marker.

"Jim, look, there it is!" I yelled. "We made it!"

God had given me the strength to reach my goal, and I hadn't even realized it. *I wonder where my strength ran out today and His began?* I thought.

When I arrived home, I took a quick bath. But the bath took so much energy in my exhausted state, it took me fifteen minutes of struggling to transfer back into the wheelchair. Wanice served up another huge meal of carbohydrates, but I was so tired I could barely eat. It was then that I realized that I needed some serious prayer before I could even consider getting back up the next morning and walking for another day. I called a few friends and asked them to come over and pray with me. While we waited, Bob and Jeff examined my open sore below my right knee. It was looking pretty bad.

My admiration for these two men was growing by the minute. They, like Jim, were demonstrating a servant's heart. They answered the phone and helped Wanice clear the table, and Jeff made some signs for our backs. Each one of them called home to tell their wives about the day; I could tell by their hushed voices that they had a great deal of concern about how I was going to be able to finish two more days of extreme physical exertion. But instead of burdening me with their concerns, they kept their worries to themselves.

About an hour later, people started arriving to pray. They formed a circle around me and got on their knees. One by one, they prayed for my strength to return the next morning.

By 9:00 P.M., everyone had left. At 9:30, I crawled into bed to sleep for seven hours, but my legs had other plans. I slept in fits and starts, only to be awakened by painful leg spasms caused by my hypersensitive nerves. It truly is ironic—I can't feel pain that would cause serious injury, such as a burn or a blister, yet out of the blue I am in agony from what amounts to "faulty wiring." Each time Wanice moved in bed, the sheets brushed up against a sensitive spot and caused pain so severe I had to bite my lip to keep from screaming. I counted the hours until morning and prayed that I would have energy upon waking.

Day Two

Buzzzz . . .

"Rob, are you awake? It's 4:30!"

"Yes, let's do it just like yesterday morning."

Wanice bounced up and woke Bob and Jeff. I could hear Bob from my room. He growled like a bear when Wanice tried to wake him, but she just laughed at him. By 5:30, we were having breakfast when Jeff noted that I looked in better shape than Bob did. We all laughed and decided that Bob was just not a morning person. By 6:00, we were in the car, and at 6:30 we were at the bottom of a hill that I would need to climb. I was anxious to see how much slower I was the second day than the first.

"Well, here goes," I said, standing up. Suddenly, a sharp pain hit me in my groin above my left leg. The muscle felt so tight and the pain didn't lessen until I slowly stretched several times. With Jeff and Bob looking on with concern, I began to walk. As I started up the hill, which didn't look nearly as steep as it had the day before, the pain slowly dissipated. Within half an hour I had reached the top. I didn't even feel as if I had walked the previous day. *Prayer works wonders,* I thought.

But what I saw disturbed me: The general slope for the entire
day was up. It wasn't a very steep grade, but it was noticeable.
I tried not to think about it. Instead, I busied my mind thinking about all of the previous night's prayers. *Just keep taking
one step at a time. Just worry about getting to the next stopping point,* I told myself again and again.

Jim, Jay, Bob, Jeff and I took one step at a time, one mile at
a time and one break at a time, knowing we had the faith to
hang on. I began taking breaks every mile instead of every
mile and a half, like the day before. While I maintained my
speed up to almost a mile an hour, I just couldn't walk as far
without a break.

At the third rest stop, a car pulled up and two men got out.
The first set of reporters had arrived to document my journey.
While one took pictures, the other asked every question imag-
inable and jotted notes on his notepad. After fifteen minutes,
Jeff looked at his watch and said we had better get moving.

Bob and Jeff changed my socks, checked my legs for sores
one more time, rubbed my aching hands and off we went once
again. The reporters walked along for fifteen or twenty minutes to ask some more questions, then took off to meet their
deadline. Around noon, we stopped for lunch at a restaurant
along the way. It couldn't have come a moment too soon. I
was beginning to drag my right leg. We had reached the
halfway mark for the day, with four more miles to go after
lunch. While we ate, another friend showed up with a video
camera to make a tape of the remainder of the walk and to eat
with us. I practically inhaled my own big meal, then started
eating the food off of everyone else's plates. I just couldn't get
enough!

After lunch, we went out to the car and took another break.

After I fell fast asleep, the guys decided to let me sleep for an hour. But by 1:30 when they woke me up, I was really tired. Plus both of my legs were tight, and my arms and back were sore. We had to move up the rest stops even more often, to every three-quarters of a mile. That distance marked the outside edge of my endurance. The truth was, it was all I could do to get from break to break. Slowing us down even further, my breaks lasted twenty minutes instead of fifteen as it took longer and longer for me to recover from the previous short walk.

As we made our way to the next rest stop, I was encouraged by people waving at us and car horns honking. Apparently they heard about the walk on the radio.

After the next break, the road returned to a flat grade and I could see the lake in the distance—the one that signaled the end of that day's walk. My hypersensitive right leg hurt so badly that I was close to tears. I was hurting all over; my right leg was just one more place. Slowly another mile went by, and the road started to dip down toward the lake. We cut across a supermarket parking lot, and as I walked past a gas station, one of the mechanics scrambled out from under a car and ran over to me.

"Are you Rob Bryant?" he asked, wiping the grease off of his hand onto his trousers.

"Yes," I answered and introduced the rest of the gang.

"I heard about what you are doing on the radio this morning. I can't believe you're trying to walk so far! It's such a pleasure to meet you. Your inspiration has given me courage to face my own problems. If you can handle your problems, surely I can handle mine. Can I do anything for you?"

"Well, to tell you the truth, I need to drink Gatorade to maintain adequate fluids in my system. We're almost out. Do you have any?"

He nodded and signaled me to wait. In less than a minute, he reappeared and handed Bob about ten free cans of Gatorade. We thanked him, said good-bye, and were off again. In less than an hour we were at the lake. I swallowed several aspirins to help block out some of the pain from my back, arms and hands. My hands were not only turning a reddish purple color from the constant pressure on the crutches, they had deep bruises in them. The problem was that I had to lift at least half of my weight on each stride in order to move my legs forward. My hands were taking a tremendous beating and were beginning to tingle with numbness. I hoped that I was not doing any permanent damage.

Although it was tough to think about, we decided that I should walk another mile on the other side of the lake so there would be less to walk on the following day. I was supposed to finish at 2:00 in Keist Park the next day—that was still eight miles to go. Jeff figured I would need to average more than a mile an hour if I stopped at the lake. We drove across the lake, and I walked one more hot, painful mile. I remembered my first mile less than a year before, especially Wanice's and the kids' faces at the door as they cheered me on. At the end of this mile, I collapsed in the car. Another day of the Miracle Walk had come to an end. It was after 6:30 P.M.

"You know that we have to be back here in less than twelve hours from now to do it again," I said, with my uncanny ability to state the obvious.

"Don't depress me with the facts. Let's go home," Bob said. We packed up our gear and drove away.

Home was a madhouse with the phone constantly ringing with calls from reporters and concerned friends. While I rested and Wanice made dinner, Bob and Jeff took over. By 8:00, I had already taken a shower, had my wounds doctored and was in bed. My friends were still busy running around, making sure everything was ready for the next day. I thanked God for sending them. My legs were spasming badly and the pain was terrific, but I was too tired to pay much attention. By 9:00, I was fast asleep and dreaming about walking across that finish line on the following day.

Day Three

By the third day we had the routine down, so when the alarm went off at 4:00 A.M., we were ready to go by 5:30. This time I felt as if I had been hit by a truck. I had no energy or motivation left. Bob went outside and brought in the newspaper. There it was, in black and white, a huge headline on the front page: MAN LEANS ON FAITH IN HIS MIRACLE WALK. I remembered who was really behind this walk and suddenly I was filled with energy. We arrived at the final starting point at 6:15 A.M., and I stretched my sore, stiff muscles.

"I've got an idea," I joked. "Why don't you guys take turns carrying me this morning? Who wants to be first?"

Everyone laughed, and I was off again, slowly this time and noticeably dragging my right leg with each stride. *Please God, just give me the strength to make it to the next break point,* I prayed silently. I blocked out the pain by listening to a radio. I listened to some of the largest radio stations in Dallas, and I heard most of them say something about my walk and what time I was supposed to finish. At around 9:00 A.M., a photographer from United Press International took pictures that would be wired all across the country. I couldn't believe that the Miracle Walk was going to get such coverage. But why shouldn't I believe it? God had promised that if I remembered Him, He would remember me. Just in case I was tempted to pat myself on the back, I made a mental note that when I finished I was going to give all of the glory to God. By 11:00 A.M., it was over 100 degrees and I was having some trouble breathing. At 11:30, we sighted a helicopter from one of the local radio stations; it continued to fly over at least once an hour to keep track of my progress.

It was noon when I arrived at the park, but I couldn't believe it. I kept looking at my watch in amazement. I had just walked six miles in six hours, and that was with two long breaks. All that was left to do was walk around the park, a mile and a half more. My arrival time was to be 2:00 P.M. While we broke for lunch, Wanice and friends put up signs and strung a finish line tape for me to walk through at the center of the park. It was exciting to see the park was getting crowded and people were gathering at the finish line. After lunch, we started again. I felt beyond exhaustion and numb. The sore below my knee was bright red despite the knee pad, but nothing was going to stop me now. I had heard runners talk about the "wall"—the point where a good runner will stop but a great runner will continue. It's when the pain is intolerable, all of your energy is gone, and your body is screaming at you to stop. Still, you just keep on going, despite the fact that it seems impossible. That's what I felt as I was halfway around the park, but I forced myself to keep walking. *Just one more step,* I would tell myself, *Just one more step.* And so I continued until I was three quarters of the way through the park. When I finally rested on a park bench, the end was in sight. *Was it true?* I thought. *Did I just walk twenty-four miles just one year from the day that I could only walk one block?* I got up and started again, saying, "Thank you, Jesus" with each step.

There it was up ahead—the finish line. A small crowd of friends, news teams and reporters cheered me on. Suddenly with fifty yards to go, a TV cameraman stood in front of me as a reporter asked me, "Why did you do this?" I began telling him of my struggle to walk again, of my faith in Jesus Christ—that He was the one who was worthy of praise. Five minutes later, I was approaching the tape, and my emotions began to well up within me. As I approached the finish line my sons, Jason and Jonathan, ran up to me and gave me a hug.

"I'm proud of you, Dad!" Jason said as he backed away for me to finish. I stopped for a second, then broke through the tape to cheers from the crowd. Right in the middle was Kent Waltrep, president of the American Paralysis Association. I was ecstatic he had come to greet me at the finish line. I caught my breath for a moment and waited for the applause to stop. Jeff handed me a handmade replica of a check he had made. I turned to Kent. It suddenly became quiet. The only sounds were the cameras clicking and rolling.

"Kent, on behalf of all the people who pledged money for this three-day Independence Day walk, I would like to present you with a check for nine thousand dollars. I do this in hope that the dollars raised here today will go toward research in finding a cure for accidental paralysis. I hope that one day you and I can walk without the aid of crutches, braces and wheelchairs."

Kent congratulated me and presented me with a plaque: "In Appreciation of His Courage and Determination, the American Paralysis Association Honors Rob Bryant for His Independence Day Walk, July 4, 1984."

"Thank you for the inspiration that you have given to hundreds of thousands of people around the country. It is people like you who will give the rest of us the courage to face our problems regardless of what they are. Thank you for the money and rest assured that we will put it to good use."

With no strength left, I asked for my wheelchair. I sat down, and the Miracle Walk was at long last over. God and I had done it.

Kent and I began to talk as a few reporters gathered around to get the story. Kent mentioned to one of them that as far as he knew this was the farthest that a paraplegic had ever walked. I tried to talk to Kent and answer all of the reporters' questions one at a time. I introduced Jim Hurst, Jeff Wilson, Bob Peterson and my wife to the press. They answered questions, too. After about a half an hour, Kent and I drove to East Dallas to an APA fund-raiser that was going on at E-Systems of Dallas. Before a crowd of about four hundred people, Kent again presented me with the plaque, and I was asked to say a few words. I was so tired that I really don't remember much of what I said, but I do remember saying this: "I want to give all of the praise and glory to God for making this walk possible. All of the hard work and determination will not rejuvenate nerves. I can move my left leg enough to walk some. But I believe it was God who gave me the strength to walk twenty-four miles. If courage is all it takes to walk after an injury like mine, Kent Waltrep would be walking, too. He certainly does not lack any determination. I also would like to thank my friends, and especially my wife, for believing in this dream of mine. Thank you all."

I again received a round of applause. Jeff, Bob, Wanice and I visited with a few people who had questions about the walk, and then we went home. I collapsed into my easy chair. During the next few hours the phone rang off the wall with news people. Cable News Network called and interviewed me. My voice was heard around the world at six o'clock that night. The rest of the night passed quickly. After setting off fireworks with family and friends, I was in bed by ten. Despite the pain, spasms and excruciating hypersensitivity, I slept well.

The following morning, I took Bob and Jeff to the airport. We said our good-byes, and I waved as my two friends boarded the plane. During the drive home, I thought about when the Miracle Walk was only a dream. What if I had decided it was impossible, and it had merely remained a dream? I would never have developed my faith, and God

Crossing the finish line of The Miracle Walk

would not have blessed me with a miracle. *Godly dreams,* I decided, *are to be realized, not merely fantasized.*

Little did I know that within two weeks I would speak to several churches, be on several TV shows and that my story would appear in more than fifty newspapers from coast to coast. The Miracle Walk was over, but the hope that it would bring to millions was only beginning. Once again God showed me that if I would take care of His business, He would take care of mine!

PART II

You Have to Crawl Before You Can Walk

Step 1

Build a
Strong Foundation

The Lord is my rock, and my fortress, and my deliverer.

                                                        −2 Samuel 22:2

The first step in overcoming adversity is to have something solid to stand on. When I began walking again, I had to learn to stand using parallel bars before receiving my braces and crutches. In other words, I had to establish a foundation upon which to stand before I could try to stand. This holds true for emotional, physical or spiritual adversity. A person who cannot follow through on anything, or who is unstable emotionally, may have a poor foundation for life. Fortunately, that does not mean that person is doomed to failure. There are certain life principles, I feel, that can act as building blocks or bricks with which you can create your own solid foundation wherever you are in your life.

I first came to understand how vital a strong foundation is while I was in college, working in construction. I learned many truths during that period: always wear my hard hat and never arm-wrestle a guy named Bubba who bends steel for a living. I also learned about concrete, buildings and foundations. Most importantly, I learned that a building needs the right foundation.

If these simple rules are not applied, the results can be disastrous. These four rules became ingrained in my way of thinking. I realized they were also good rules to apply to life.

Rule Number One: The Foundation Must Be Built on Solid Ground

So many times builders have made the mistake of building on unstable ground. The Tower of Pisa is a monumental reminder of this truth. People have built their homes on the sides of mountains, and each year we read about mudslides in California and how many homes go down with them. In order to build a solid structure, the foundation must be anchored to solid rock. This is accomplished with the use of pylons. Pylons are columns of concrete, which are poured into deep holes, which tie the foundation to the rock beneath the surface.

In life the same rule applies. We must build our life on solid ground. Many scriptures and parables deal with this simple yet profound truth. People can be completely devastated by life's trials because of a lack of adequate foundation. Trials either make us stronger or destroy us. Think of the terrible devastation of a tornado, fire, earthquake or flood. Some people recover remarkably, rebuilding within a year, while others seem never to recover from the catastrophe. Our ability to cope with certain situations rests on our foundation.

We all have voids in our lives that we try to fill, but I believe there is only one entity that will truly fill these voids, these holes in the foundation, if you will. Money, power and fame will not do. There are those who have accumulated millions of dollars, yet it's still not enough for them. They have everything life can offer, yet it's not sufficient to satisfy their hunger for more. It is as though they are searching for just one more possession. They think that if they can get just one more "thing," they will be happy. Yet, when they have it, they realize it is not enough either, and the search to fill the void—

maybe with alcohol, risky behaviors, food, shopping or what-ever—continues.

How many apparently "successful" people in this world end up leading empty lives or committing suicide? The end comes when they ask the question, "Is this all there is to life?"

There are cults that prey on the minds of young people who are growing and searching for their place in life, kids who just want to be loved and feel a sense of belonging. These kids usually come from dysfunctional homes and are looking for someone to love and appreciate them. Without the right foundation, these young people are drawn in. These cults often take everything they have. They take their money, their possessions, and given the opportunity, their minds.

This same principle operates within gangs. Kids who are lost, who don't feel any love or respect from their families, or don't feel any allegiance to their school or a church, or anything else, are ripe for the picking by gang leaders. They target children and teens who feel alienated from everyone else and build them up with a false sense of security and belonging. By the time they're done with these innocent kids, they have them in their control and convinced that no one else cares for them except the gang. This is the foundation or basis of building a criminal.

Rule Number Two: The Foundation Must Be Correct for the Base of the Building

This seems simple enough yet many people violate this premise. For instance, an all-too-common phenomenon is the workaholic. Workaholics build their entire lives on the foundation of their jobs. They give work all of their time and energy. As they make more money and receive more power, they get drawn in even more. It is the single most important thing in their lives. The years pass, and soon they are middle-aged and alone. Their families have either left them, or their kids are already grown and have families of their own. Soon these workaholics move into their sixties and retire, and the foundation of their life—the job—is gone. They move beyond the periphery of the job foundation and their life crumbles. How many times have we seen this personality type die shortly after retiring? Ensure the foundation for your life is big enough for your building. It must hold you, your family, your goals and the rest of your life.

Rule Number Three: The Foundation Must Be Strong Enough to Hold the Weight

This is rudimentary enough, but it is without a doubt the most deceptive principle. A foundation may look very strong. Yet, if basic rules are not followed, it won't be hardy enough for the weight of the structure. For instance, the foundation must be poured when the temperature is correct. There has to be enough rock and steel added, and it has to be thick enough. If not, it will not hold the weight. Oftentimes we find ourselves testing our foundations like the unwise little boy who tests the ice on the pond early in the winter. He steps onto it and then jumps off. He doesn't hear any cracks, so he tries it again. Once more, nothing appears to be alarming, so the boy puts on his skates and races to the middle of the pond. He glides along for several minutes when the ice begins cracking all around. The ice held his weight for awhile, but his jumping and twirling began fatiguing the ice. Within seconds it breaks beneath him, and he plunges into the icy waters below. If we try looking for suitable foundations for our lives by this method, we will very likely receive an abrupt surprise.

Rule Number Four: Once We Have the Right Foundation, We Need to Build the Right Structure

If you construct the building out of hay and stubble, when fire comes (and it will come), it will all burn away. The fire will leave a perfectly good foundation, but the building will be gone. Similarly, if you are absolutely devastated each time there is a tragedy in your life, this may describe your building. You function fine, but each time you are shaken, you crumble. However, if you build your house out of gold and precious metals, the building will actually be purified by fire (trials). It will become more durable, and thus more valuable, each time it is exposed to fire. For instance, I have much more confidence sitting in my wheelchair than many of my colleagues who are running around perfectly "healthy." I know who I am and why I am valuable because my building has been tested by fire.

I survived this test because of my faith in God and because I had a solid foundation which was built years before.

Click-Click-Click:
The Life and Death Meter

"You can't catch me now," I screamed with excitement as I ran away from my older brother Mike. Mike was ten years old (a year older than I) and much stronger, but I could usually out-run him. I had to run to survive because Mike was so much stronger and bigger than I was. This was an event we had been looking forward to for months. Now it was here. We were actu-ally at the 1964 World's Fair in New York City. We were com-pletely surrounded by people shuffling past us as we ran past several long lines of people. Mike and I knew where to meet Mom and Dad later, so we didn't worry about getting lost.

I was outrunning Mike as I dodged through the crowds, when suddenly I saw something that stopped me dead in my tracks. I had no idea what it was, but somehow I knew it was important. There hanging high above me were two enormous analog-type meters. It was not common to see huge meters in the sixties and maybe that's what stopped me at first. But the more I looked at them, the more captivated I was. Both of them were clicking out numbers. The numbers were astro-nomically large to my little mind and were somewhere in the billions. One was turning over numbers slightly faster than the other, but they were counting something very quickly. What could they be counting? Mike caught up with me and was about to "pound" me, when he saw the meters, too. Just like me, he turned his full attention to them. We both stood there and watched the meters as if we were in a trance. There were two simple signs hanging over the meters. Each of the signs just had one word on them. The meter that was clicking slightly faster said Birth, the other said Death. The meaning of every click profoundly affected me. Each time one of the meters clicked, it meant a life had either begun or ended.

At my young age, I thought my life was the center of the universe. Everyone else was just passing through with little impact to what really mattered—me. I suddenly realized my

entire life was just another click on the meters. One click
brought me into life; the other would take me out. It made me
realize how small and insignificant my life really was. My
entire life represented only one click out of the billions on the
meter. What about all the other clicks? Each click of the meter
was a life that was no more or less important than my own.
With each click, a child was born somewhere. *Who was he or
she? What would that child's life be like? What would that
child be when he or she grew up?* I wondered who they were
supposed to be or what they were to accomplish.

As I stood there pondering these questions, my mind traveled back in time to a significant event in our house; nevertheless, it was just another click on the meter.

A Child Is Born

"Here is your little brother," my mother said as she placed
the little bundle in front of Mike and me. Somewhere deep
inside the blankets was Steve, our newborn brother.

Mom was a conscientious mother who read books about
child-rearing. You know, the type of book you read, try a few
of the author's suggestions, then throw it away saying, "The
author either did not have children or has never met mine."

This particular book said there were several ways to reduce
sibling rivalries (obviously the author did not have brothers or
sisters). One of them was to lay the baby down in front of the
other children, then explain a few ground rules of what not to
touch, and leave the children alone to get to know each other.
Mom explained not to touch the soft part of Steve's head. This

seemed funny to me. If Steve's head was as hard as my older brother's was, a jackhammer couldn't hurt it. Besides, a Bryant with a soft head was an oxymoron. Mom left the room, and Mike and I looked at each other, then at our little brother. Tiny Steve had no idea how vulnerable he really was in this situation. We slowly unwrapped the cocoonlike bundle. It was like shucking corn. When shucking corn, you remove everything that does not look like corn. In this case we just removed everything that didn't look like Steve. We looked at his little arms and legs, then at his head and feet. This methodical evaluation was going fine until Mike made a startling discovery.

"There's a piece of string hanging from his stomach," Mike said matter-of-factly.

Sure enough, there it was. It was protruding from his navel. Mike knew that he himself did not have a piece of string hanging from his navel. Therefore, not wanting a defective little brother, he began gently pulling on the string. Mike stopped pulling and was contemplating his next move with his hand still on the string. There had to be a way to remove it from Steve's otherwise unblemished body. Mom, who had been secretly (and wisely) watching our every move, saw what was happening (and what could potentially happen), and rushed back into the room.

"Stop! Mike, don't do that!" she screamed as she ran toward us.

Luckily, Mom reached Steve in time before any damage was done. My mind came back to the present. I realized how close Steve could have come to clicking both of the meters within the same week.

The "Stormy" Night

Another birth experience from my childhood came to mind, as I stood frozen in time and space staring at the meter. Some of my most cherished memories as a child were the times I spent on the back of a horse. Stormy was her name and she was a big black mare that most children only dream about having. How I had acquired the horse is a story of its own and will be discussed later. But one of the pinnacle events during my years with Stormy was when we bred her with a large Arabian stud. We all anxiously awaited the day she would deliver her foal. Stormy was my pride and joy, and I was as nervous as she was. On one of the veterinarian's regular visits to see Stormy, he pronounced she would give birth within the following twenty-four hours. I actually felt like an expectant father and paced back and forth as much as she did. Later that night, I asked Mom if I could sleep in the barn with Stormy. I wanted to be there if she needed help, and my mom agreed as long as I did not get too close when the actual birth was going on.

"If Stormy gets too nervous, she could kick you and hurt you and the foal," Mom warned.

I knew there was no use in trying to change Mom's mind, and I agreed to the terms. Besides, as zealous as I was to join Stormy in the barn, I knew Mom was right. At dusk I grabbed a sleeping bag and headed for the barn. Stormy was very nervous, but my presence seemed to calm her down. I laid out fresh straw and hay for Stormy to use. When I lay down on the opposite side of the barn, she walked over to me. She nudged me with her nose, and I gently petted her head and rubbed her neck. As soon as I touched her, much of the stress left her body. It seemed that, as long as I was touching her, she was fine. The hours passed, and I eventually fell asleep with Stormy standing close by my side.

Just about daybreak, I heard a sound. It was a low guttural snorting sound. I opened my eyes, and Stormy was standing across the barn beside the hay. The barn was very dark, but the sun was rising, so it was getting lighter by the minute. I walked over to the barn door and turned on a small light, but I kept my distance from Stormy. I slowly returned to my sleeping bag and watched. I could tell by Stormy's watchful eye that she did not want me too close to her anyway. She was standing sideways to me, so I was in a wonderful position to watch the whole miraculous process.

Within minutes, the foal was slipping out. Stormy was obviously in pain, yet stood very still. Within a few more minutes, the foal was on the ground. With a loving touch of her nose, Stormy began inspecting her foal. I named her Misty! Misty was absolutely beautiful and possessed a jet-black coat just like her mom. Stormy cleaned Misty and protected her from any outside hindrances. Even though Stormy knew me well, she was still an animal who would protect her baby any way she could if she felt I was a threat. Within hours, Misty stood for the first time and took her first wobbly steps.

By mid-morning, Stormy allowed me to pet Misty for the first time. It was the proudest I had ever seen Stormy. She held her head high and pranced around like a million-dollar thoroughbred. I was honored that she let me share the moment with her.

"Click, click, click . . ."

My mind returned to the meter and I realized the clicking was still continuing. While I had been standing there thinking

about Stormy, hundreds of lives had begun and ended. As profound as the birth of Misty was to me, it was not even a click
on this meter. No, the clicks here meant people with souls
were being born. *Who were they? What were their names?*
Would their lives be happy or sad?

The numbers continued to click on the meters. My gaze
went from the birth to the death meter. I had little experience
with death at that age. I knew it meant the end of life, as we
know it. I saw my maternal grandfather in a casket a few years
before. I remember thinking how old he looked. He had suffered for as long as I had known him. I remembered my
mother saying, "It's a blessing" and "He's in a better place
now." I wasn't sure what she meant at the time. It did make me
feel better, however, to think he was better off somehow.

The Great Flood

I did not have another close encounter with death until years
later in high school. I was seventeen and death was the furthest
thing from my mind, but death was in the air. There had been
a massive flood in the area. Martial law was declared, reserve
troops were called in, and citizens were asked to help their
neighbors. I was assigned to a patrol that helped stranded
people get to higher ground. My older brother, Mike, and I
helped people move through the deep water to a college on top
of a hill. I'm sorry to say a few people were never found, and
several others did not survive.

A makeshift hospital was prepared at the college. As Mike
and I worked feeding a small crowd of people, I noticed a

coroner zipping up a body bag. I looked at the body bag. I couldn't help thinking I could have been in one of the bags. The question, *Why this person and not me?* occurred to me. Soon other questions followed in my mind: *Why did she have to die in the first place? Who was she? Did she die quickly or painfully?*

Several weeks later, after the floodwaters had receded, most everything was back to normal, although the mud and water damage took months to repair. I worked as a janitor and security guard at a mall and one day I noticed an older man sitting on a bench. He was just staring off into space. He was prematurely gray but the lines and wrinkles on his face gave him the appearance of being ancient. He looked as if he had not slept in days and his clothes were wrinkled and dirty. He had a look of total defeat on his face. Each time I passed, he appeared to be more despondent and distant.

I made the last pass for the night before my shift was over. As I walked past him the final time, I watched him as he slowly slumped over and fell to the floor. I tried to reach him before his head hit the floor, but I didn't make it. I checked his pulse immediately, but I could not find it. I called an ambulance and they were there within minutes. They tried in vain to revive him. A coroner took him away, and it wasn't until days later when I read an article about the old man that I discovered what had really killed him. It was a broken heart. I read that he had lost his farm and one of his children in the flood. The man literally decided to die.

"Click, click, click . . ."

My mind went back to the meter at the World's Fair. A life had tragically ended, yet it only represented one click on the meter. *Was there no fuller meaning in life than just a click on a meter? Was our world just the result of a Big Bang in space? Did microorganisms, then finally vertebrates, follow the bang?* This concept left me feeling empty and cold. *Was there nothing more to life? Was my entire life no more than two clicks?* I wrestled with this question for years afterward. The clicking meters haunted me. It was as if I could hear them click in the background. In my mind's eye, I saw the celebration of life only to be followed by the pain of death. It seemed so futile.

Several years later, I would wrestle with those clicks one more time before making Jesus Christ the foundation of my life. That's when a brand-new world opened up to me. I saw the meters for what they were. The clicks in fact marked the beginning and end of life. What we choose to do between the clicks is up to us. God has a beautiful plan for my life. So far it has led me over mountains, to more than thirty countries and through incredible adventures. My life has been filled with wonders beyond description. I know one day I'll hear my own click. What a glorious day that will be! I will leave my wheelchair and crutches behind and be as whole as everybody else once again. The click-click-click of the two meters no longer haunts me. Instead I see them as God sending me to earth, and then bringing me back home.

There is only one foundation that is built on solid ground and big enough for the base of the building. It is strong enough to hold the weight. That foundation is Jesus Christ. The first step in defeating adversity is to have a foundation to stand on. Only you can decide what that foundation will be. But remember, the house you build will only be as strong as the foundation on which it sits. What do you want the "clicks" of your life to represent, and how will you make this happen? Could it be that you need a stronger foundation?

In order to discover this foundation, I suggest you do the following:

- Surround yourself with others who have sound foundations for their lives. No one is strong enough to stand alone. If you cut yourself off from others, you will fail. But avoid people who are bitter or negative, unless you are far enough along in your own recovery that you think you can help turn them around. Usually when you're knee-deep in coping with your own problems, it's unrealistic to think your attitude won't be affected by other people's negativity.

- Ask your friends to help you assess your life and the areas in which you need stability. It is in those areas that you especially need to build on a strong foundation.

- Finally, there are times when our foundation feels so shaken, we need to ask for professional help. If depression or discouragement continually plagues your life, you may need a doctor's help. You may need to speak with a psychologist or psychiatrist, a minister, a priest, a rabbi, or a social worker. This is not a sign of weakness; it's part of taking care of yourself and your family.

READER/CUSTOMER CARE SURVEY

BA1

6757058862

We care about your opinions. Please take a moment to fill out this Reader Survey card and mail it back to us. As a special **"thank you"** we'll send you exciting news about interesting books and a valuable **Gift Certificate**

Please PRINT using ALL CAPITALS

Name

First _____ MI.⊔ Last _____ Name

Address _____

City _____ ST ⊔ Zip _____

Phone # (⊔⊔) _____ - _____ Fax # (⊔⊔) _____ - _____

Email _____

(1) Gender:
○ Female
○ Male

(2) Age:
○ 13-19 ○ 40-49
○ 20-29 ○ 50-59
○ 30-39 ○ 60+

(3) Your children's age(s):
Please fill in all that apply.
○ 6 or Under ○ 15-18
○ 7-10 ○ 19+
○ 11-14

(8) Marital Status:
○ Married
○ Single
○ Divorced / Widowed

(9) Was this book:
○ Purchased For Yourself?
○ Received As a Gift?

(10)How many HCI books have you bought or read?
○ 1 ○ 3
○ 2 ○ 4+

(11) Did this book meet your expectations?
○ Yes
○ No

(12) How did you find out about this book? *Please fill in ONE.*
○ Personal Recommendation
○ Store Display
○ TV/Radio Program
○ Bestseller List
○ Website
○ Advertisement/Article or Book
○ Catalog or Mailing
○ Other _____

(13) What FIVE subject areas do you enjoy reading about most? *Rank only FIVE. Choose 1 for your favorite, 2 for second favorite, etc.*

	1	2	3	4	5
Self Development	○	○	○	○	○
Parenting	○	○	○	○	○
Spirituality/Inspiration	○	○	○	○	○
Family and Relationships	○	○	○	○	○
Health and Nutrition	○	○	○	○	○
Recovery	○	○	○	○	○
Business/Professional	○	○	○	○	○
Entertainment	○	○	○	○	○
Sports	○	○	○	○	○
Teen Issues	○	○	○	○	○
Pets	○	○	○	○	○

BA1

(25) Are you:
○ A Parent?
○ A Grandparent

9396058864

(18) Where do you purchase most of your books?
Please fill in your top TWO choices only.
○ General Bookstore
○ Religious Bookstore
○ Warehouse / Price Club
○ Discount or Other Retail Store
○ Website
○ Book Club / Mail Order

(20) What type(s) of magazines do you SUBSCRIBE to?
Fill in up to FIVE categories.
○ Parenting
○ Sports
○ Fashion
○ Business / Professional
○ World News / Current Events
○ General Entertainment
○ Homemaking, Cooking, Crafts
○ Women's Issues
○ Other (please specify) _____

Step 2

Realize That Life Isn't Fair But You Affect the Outcome

Life is like a box of chocolates; you never know what you are going to get.

—Forrest Gump

Life Isn't Fair

This is one rule that's absolutely true and applies to everyone, no matter what their situation in life. You can become bitter and wallow in self-pity if you don't realize this, wasting your days complaining that it isn't fair that you are so sick, miserable, unlucky, poor, unloved, whatever.

Instead, accept this rule as a fact of life and start looking at all the positives in your life. Concentrate on the things you *can* do, and do them well! Don't worry about the things you can't do or have no control over. This will only serve to make you bitter and will stop your growth as a person. In my opinion, self-pity can stop us quicker than any other thought process! We can begin thinking thoughts like: "People don't expect me to do well. I am not nearly as smart as Betty is. I'm not nearly as strong as John is. I am not nearly as beautiful as Janet is. My disability or addiction is worse than George's." But what would it change? Will I walk again or regain full control of my body because I think, "Poor me. No one has it so bad?" Of course not! Ask yourself, "What is self-pity going to do to help me?" Believe me, it is not going to help. It only serves to take you further down the road to depression and despair. I find that the days I decide to feel sorry for myself (these days are very infrequent), I stop dreaming and setting daily goals. If I let self-pity stop me from having some sort of goal for the day, I become paralyzed! I can look at myself in terms of what I have and use it, or I can look at what I don't have. I could allow myself to be bitter or feel self-pity over the fact that I cannot walk and others can. Yet if I think in terms of jealousy about the talents and abilities of others, I may never accomplish what I am capable of accomplishing. I choose to look at what I can do. I can use my arms, my brain, my self-reliance, confidence and hundreds of other positive attributes to accomplish my goals. I set two World Records by concentrating on the things over which I had control.

Years ago, I tried to explain this concept to my eight-year-old son Jonathan, who was filled with self-pity.

❀   ❀   ❀

"Dad, it's not fair," Jonathan screamed.

"What's not fair, Son?"

"Jason gets to spend the night at Grandma's house and see two cousins, too. The last time I spent the night there, nobody was there except Grandma and Grandpa. It's just not fair!"

I thought about his statement for a moment and shocked him when I agreed with him.

"You're right, Son. It's not fair. Whoever said everything in life is going to be fair?"

"Dad, you don't understand!"

"I do understand, Son. You think if Jason gets to do something you don't get to do, it's not fair."

"Yeah, that's right, Dad; it's not fair."

"Son, if everything in life was fair, would we need the police? Would we need laws and judges? There are going to be times when life just is not fair. For instance, a few years ago I was up for a promotion. A man was promoted who did not know half as much as I did about the job. But he knew the right people. That was not fair, either, but it happened just the same."

"Yeah, but you're my dad. You're supposed to protect me when life isn't fair."

I reflected back to a time I remembered telling my father life was unfair.

I said to Jonathan, "Son, when I was twelve years old, I had the most incredible dog. He was a combination of collie and German shepherd. His name was Lad. He outweighed most other dogs, and they wanted no part of him. I once saw him chase off several wild dogs without hesitation. He was also a great hunter. He was fearless and aggressive when it came to hunting, yet very gentle with the family. He was also a good watchdog. If someone approached whom he did not know, he growled and was always prepared to protect us. He was the dog most little boys wanted as a pet. Once, while walking through the woods together, he dove in front of me to block the assault of a surprised raccoon. Lad waited until I was clear before running away from the animal to safety himself. I hugged him, and he just wagged his tail. He licked me as if to say, 'I know you would do the same for me.' We would hunt by the hour together, and we became as close as two differing species could be to each other. However, something happened that changed all of that forever.

"I was riding my bike down the road, and Lad was following me. It was a beautiful fall day, just right for riding and looking at the scenery. The leaves were beginning to change, and the mountains were ablaze with every possible shade of red, yellow, green and brown. We were traveling like the wind, and he was keeping up with me. Just then, a large dog ran out to the edge of the opposite side of the road. Lad ran across the road to cut off this dog's path to me. Lad hit the dog with his large chest and sent the other dog rolling across the yard. Lad was not satisfied with the victory and leaped on the disoriented dog and grabbed him by the throat without actually biting him. He was proving the point he could kill that dog any time he wanted. The other dog yelped surrender and offered his stomach and upraised paws in a gesture of total surrender. I was not sure if Lad was going to release his death grip on the other dog."

"What did you do, Dad?" Jonathan asked, wide-eyed.

"I yelled across the road for him to come to me. By this time, I had already jumped off my bike and was waiting for him to catch up.

"Lad heard my call and immediately released the dog and headed toward me. Lad was so trusting of my call that he didn't bother to look either way for traffic; unfortunately, neither did I. As Lad came running straight toward me, I suddenly saw a car coming out of the corner of my eye. Everything appeared to go into slow motion as the car bore down on Lad. With too little time to react, all the driver could do was swerve and hit his brakes. It was too late! The bumper hit Lad with such force that Lad flew through the air across the road. He landed on the shoulder of the road with a thud. Lad tried to get up but immediately fell back on his side. He whimpered quietly. When I got to his side, I saw that he was very weak. Lad just looked up into my eyes as if asking for my help. He had done so many things for me, now it was my turn. But I was powerless to help him! The last thing Lad did before he died was to lick my hand."

"That's so sad," Jonathan said.

"I know. I remember crying out 'It's not fair!' I began to cry uncontrollably as the driver of the car stopped to offer me a ride home. The poor man stood there looking down at me knowing he had killed my dog. A tear ran down his cheek as I continued to cry. I could not believe my old friend was dead. I didn't blame the driver for hitting my dog, but I couldn't force myself to ride with him, either. The poor man stood there, closing his eyes. I picked up Lad in my arms. His head fell limply to the side. He was very heavy, but I carried him the half-mile home. I laid Lad gently down by the back door and ran into the house crying. Mom tried unsuccessfully to console me. I told her how I had called his name to come back across the road to me. Lad trusted me and now he was dead. 'I killed my dog, Mom,' I said. 'It's not fair! It's not fair!'"

The memory was so clear that I relived the moment as I talked to Jonathan. Suddenly, my mind was back in the present and I was looking at my son.

"Son, did I kill my dog? No, of course not. All I know is that I did not understand why my dog had to die. One detail I was sure of, however, was that it was not fair. Son, have you ever noticed there are two kinds of older people in the world? There are those who have grown bitter at unfair events that happened to them. They become negative and distrusting of everything and everyone. On the other hand, some pick up the pieces and go on. The latter type has the ability to be content after the most terrible circumstances. The difference between these people is the same difference between the oak tree and the pine tree. The oak tree is large and majestic, but it is inflexible. If the wind blows hard enough, it will break. The pine tree, on the other hand, is flexible and gives way to the wind. It does not break, it just bends. Son, be flexible. When the winds of adversity blow, just bend with them."

I'm not sure if Jonathan understood everything I tried to teach him, but he agreed that sometimes life is just not fair.

*   *   *

The story about my dog, Lad, is tragic. It serves to illustrate the point that often we are caught in situations of total helplessness. What we do with those situations depends entirely on us. We can feel sorry for ourselves or we can go on and make the best of a bad situation. Self-pity will paralyze you whether the situation is minor or tragic!

Overcoming some types of adversity requires a new set of actions. Step back and take a look at your life from a new perspective. Ask your friends what they think. Ask your pastor. Try new approaches to new problems.

When I found myself in my wheelchair, my old solutions no longer worked. I had to get creative. Don't become so routine or unimaginative in your thinking that you always hide, use caution or, conversely, always take chances. There is a time for all three. Adversity happens not as a result of making wrong decisions (since all of us will at some point make mistakes), but from failing to use the decision-making process creatively. Of course, no action at all is worse than the lack of creativity. So get going first, and use creativity second! You can only turn a ship once it is moving. Invariably, moving in some direction is better than no movement at all. Don't allow the harsh realities of life dictate your failure!

What I'm about to say may sound harsh, but it's true. We all have our own disabilities or personal stumbling blocks. If you continue to feel sorry for yourself, you are destined to be all alone, because no one else feels sorry for you for very long. Your friends have problems of their own. Some of them will help you when you are discouraged. If, however, self-pity becomes a lifestyle, you will be very lonely! Say to yourself, *I am not going to pity myself anymore. I am going to concentrate on the things I know I can do, and I will do them to the best of my abilities.*

Change Your Perception

Is the glass half full or half empty? Do you perceive yourself as a good person or a bad person? Are you blessed or cursed?

Your perception either gives you strength or takes it away. Perception can either paralyze you or liberate you every hour of your life. My perception of my physical paralysis has allowed me to accomplish many things because I don't limit myself to what others think I am capable of doing. If you perceive that a task is going to be difficult, it probably will be. On the other hand, if you perceive a task to be easy, it will be less difficult. Doctors have understood for years that if they can convince a patient that they are receiving a painkiller, the patient will feel less pain. The placebo effect has been an accepted scientific fact for years. It actually began during the Civil War. The difference is perception.

My perception is that God has empowered me to accomplish the dreams He gives me. I will live approximately 663,936 hours. That doesn't seem like very many to me. I am going to use all of them to the fullest. If I perceive myself as a paraplegic incapable of simple tasks, I will be limited by that perception. I choose to perceive myself as a person capable of incredible things.

Self-pity can drain you of your hope. Without hope we have no reason to live. Don't let another day of self-pity paralyze you from dreaming and being all you can be. I want you to think about something. Because you are unique, you think and act differently from everyone else. Because of that uniqueness, there is something you can do better than everyone else. You need to discover that something and do it! I guarantee that if I can do it, you can do it, too!

Self-confidence comes as you achieve your goals. Begin with small goals you know you can achieve, and then continue to let your goals and dreams grow as your self-confidence grows. Soon you will not associate accomplishing your goals with self-confidence. It will just be a way of life.

You can look at yourself in one of two ways. If you look at what you have and use it, you are on the way to overcoming adversity. On the other hand, if you feel sorry for yourself and look at your weaknesses, you may never accomplish what you are actually capable of.

Here are a few helpful steps to begin overcoming self-pity.

- Give yourself time to recover from adversity. It takes time to heal after any traumatic experience. It took me

months to develop a good attitude after becoming a paraplegic. Give yourself time to cry, get angry and recover.
My wife Wanice was obviously greatly affected by my
adversity. With two babies to raise and, for a time, an
invalid husband struggling to survive, she faced her own
trials. As is typical with many women, she was so busy
day to day that she didn't have time to come to terms with
her own depression until it reared its ugly head a number
of years later. But it was inevitable that she would have to
face it and work through the grief of "what might have
been."

- Make a list of your talents. You will be encouraged as you
  record all of your talents and see how long the list is.

- Take small steps toward looking at life in a positive manner. Go a whole hour without complaining. If you can do
  this, then try it all morning. Eventually, do it for a whole
  day. Make a game out of it. Tell your friends you will pay
  them a quarter every time they hear you say something
  negative. If you are a parent of a negative child, you can
  reverse this and pay your child a quarter every time he or
  she says something positive and take quarters away
  when your child says something negative. See how many
  quarters your child has at the end of the day. I tried this
  with friends before, and it can not only be hilarious, it can
  be very revealing as to how positive or negative you are.
  You may not even realize how you are sabotaging your
  own success with a negative attitude until you do this kind
  of exercise.

- Self-pity is often a result of always looking within yourself.
  Look outwards. Help others reach their goals or help them
  with their problems. It is amazing how this will help you

with your problems. For instance, one of the best ways to banish the holiday blues is to help someone with their holiday by donating gifts at Christmas or food for a shelter at Thanksgiving.

- Sometimes our problems seem overwhelming. Whenever possible, take time out to get away from your problem and watch a beautiful sunrise, appreciate a sunset or watch the trees blow in the wind. When we get in tune with nature, it's easier to appreciate the everyday miracles in our own lives.

- Look around. It is very easy to find others less fortunate than you. The next time you're ready to have a good wallow in self-pity, think of some of them. Then thank God for all of your blessings, and say a prayer that He gives them the strength to cope with their misfortunes. It's a matter of perspective.

- Make a list of all of the things you don't like in your life. List things like your attitude, your job, your relationship with your family, etc. Now scratch out the things that you have no power over. What's left are the *many* things you *do* have the power to change.

- Finally, if you have had a negative attitude for years, give yourself time to change. When a small obstacle is in your way that would normally give you a negative attitude, decide you are going to be positive just this one time. At first this will be just an act of your will and may seem out of character for you. If you can practice by maintaining a positive attitude through a small negative event, you'll find keeping your spirit up for the bigger obstacles will become easier. Give yourself time to change old habits. You can be positive! You secretly want to be positive. All of your heroes are probably positive. (Ever hear of a superhero called Whineyman or The Complainer or The Failure? I didn't think so.) Emulate your heroes and seek inspiration from what they've overcome.

Step 3

Have Mercy
(On Yourself and Others)

Fresh courage take! The clouds that you so surely dread are big with mercy and shall break in blessings on your head.

—Old hymn

Practice What You Preach

In chapter 3, you read about the visiting nurse who left me with the hot water running in my bathtub. Her mistake caused second-degree burns to my feet and calves and set my walking progress back several months. While I could have been very angry and bitter about it, I wasn't. I was very discouraged, but never angry.

Some people might wonder why I didn't sue the nursing service for her serious mistake. Suing the service seemed hateful to me and would have done nothing to help me physically or emotionally. I would not have been able to sleep at night if I sued the nurse or the service over an accident. But I felt a duty to tell her employer what happened. When I found out that she had lost her job because of the incident, I felt terrible. So I went to the nursing service and asked them to rehire her, which they did. I'm certain she'll never make such a mistake again, to be sure. How can we expect mercy ourselves, if we are not willing to grant mercy to others?

The Merciful Rancher

Several years ago, my family and I went to the Fort Worth Stock Show. The stock show was worth attending because of all the sheep, horses, cattle, pigs, poultry, rabbits and other livestock on display. From the tiniest little bunny to the most massive Brahma bull, the owners proudly exhibit their prized animals. But for most of the owners, their animal is more of a pet and family member than a mere show animal. I loved seeing the pride in the eyes of the young 4-H members as they paraded around the ring. It is a phenomenon to behold and warms the heart.

On this particular day, we toured the various buildings and even saw camels, ostriches, emu and llamas that were being raised for profit on many farms and ranches throughout America. Before leaving, we walked past a ring where young people were parading their bulls around on a leash. I marveled at the fact that these animals outweighed their masters ten times over, yet willingly followed their beloved master around the ring led by a single small leash. One by one, the children would walk in, parade around, sell their bull to the ranchers and then leave. The ranchers filled the place and were bidding on these prize animals. The young people were excited for two reasons. First, their bulls were being bought for breeding purposes, which meant that they would not have to worry about seeing their family member between a McDonald's bun. Second, they were recouping the money that they invested during the months or years of preparation. They had fed, groomed, cared for, and sacrificed time and money for this one shining moment. One by one, they paraded around the ring and sold their animal to the ranchers who bid by the pound. The ranchers bid on what they saw with an experienced eye for cattle.

Just as we were about to leave, we saw something that was so different from the norm that we stayed a little longer. A young man walked into the ring dragging just the leash behind him.

"Can I call your attention to the front ring?" the announcer said.

This was not necessary, of course, because all eyes were staring at this young man, and the sound of the crowd died to almost silence. He was standing there looking down at his feet with the most dejected and melancholy expression on his face. He was almost in tears as the announcer continued.

"Yesterday, this young man's bull won second in the all-round competition. His bull was a magnificent animal. However, last night in his stall, the bull's neck became tangled in a leash. The bull broke its leg while struggling to free itself. It had to be destroyed, but we are going to sell his bull anyway. We are going to sell the bull despite the fact that you can't use it for breeding. You can't even have the beef because it has already been disposed of."

There was nothing but silence as everyone stared in horror at this poor, dejected young man. Everyone's heart went out to him. But what could be done to ease his pain? Would anyone actually bid hard-earned dollars for an animal that could not be used, for one that was essentially invisible? The silence was broken as the announcer proceeded.

"Let's start the bidding at fifty cents per pound."

A hand slowly raised.

"Do I hear one dollar per pound?"

Another hand was raised a little faster than the first.

"Do I hear two dollars per pound?"

A third hand went up. The bidding continued at an even faster pace. I could not believe what I was seeing and neither could the young man. He slowly looked up as a tear ran down his face. What he was seeing was mercy from total strangers. The look on his face said it all! The feeling of love, compassion and mercy was so thick you could cut it with a knife. The bidding continued to climb until the dead animal sold for over four dollars per pound (approximately eight thousand dollars!).

After it was over, I spoke to one of the ranchers who had bid on the animal. I had to ask the obvious question.

"Why did you bid on a bull you couldn't use for breeding, or even sell for beef?"

He looked at me with a look of pure compassion.

"Young man, I own a lot of land and cattle. I live in West Texas where rain is life. I learned a long time ago, that as I am merciful to others, God is merciful to me. For instance, after being merciful, I have seen a rain cloud stop over my property, rain for awhile, then move on. Besides, what good does it do me if I can't share my plenty with a young man who has nothing? I'm not talking about charity. That young man worked very hard and deserved a reward. I will sleep well tonight. Even more importantly, that young man over there will sleep well, too, knowing that someone cares."

Be merciful. As you are merciful, God and others will be merciful to you. Don't be too hard on yourself. Everyone makes mistakes; everyone faces failure. But God is a forgiving God—all you have to do is ask.

Step 4

Overcome
Your Fears

You gain strength, courage and confidence by every experience in which you really stop to look fear in the face. You are able to say to yourself, "I have lived through this horror. I can take the next thing that comes along." . . . You must do the thing you think you cannot do.

—*Eleanor Roosevelt*

The Greatest Fear

The price of not overcoming your fears can cost you everything. As you know, a piece of faulty equipment sent me falling fifty-five feet, nearly killed me and left me physically paralyzed. Yet, in spite of this, I have overcome my fear of heights—and the possibility of faulty equipment—in order to fulfill my obligations in life. In my job, I literally fly all over the world at the height of 33,000 feet in a piece of metal (like the metal pulley that forever changed my life), and I routinely fly on helicopters. Several times since my injury, I have gone downhill mono-skiing with my son, Jonathan, where I ascend high snow-covered peaks strapped into a chair-like apparatus that's dangling from a ski-lift by what looks to be a thread. While I could spend the ride up the mountain listening to my fears: *"People die every year falling out of these things," "What if the pulley snaps?"* I don't. Instead, I focus on what is important rather than the fear: *"This is the price I have to pay to ski with my son."* While I could allow my fear to stop me from being with my son, I make the conscious decision to concentrate on Jonathan instead of the fear. If you focus on the fear, you will lose every time.

When confronting a difficult situation, try to change your focus to anything else that is important to you in that moment, or that distracts you. Don't we intuitively do this when we distract ourselves by people-watching in a doctor's office or hospital waiting room when waiting for news about ourselves or a loved one? The next time you are facing a fear, step back and "visit yourself the waiting room." You will be amazed at how this change in perspective can change your reaction to the situation. Notice I said *your reaction,* not the situation. For example, two people can be in the same raft traversing mighty rapids. One of them is having a great time, yet the other person is scared to death. As you "raft though the rapids of fear," try visiting yourself. You can either be overcome by fear, or you can let out a scream and have a blast. Either way, it will not change the fact that you are in the rapids. I experienced this firsthand in July of 1983.

Against the Current

Just seven months after my injury, I joined several friends for a rafting trip on the Guadalupe River in Central Texas. As I stood on the steep banks, I noticed the water rushing past. While the others tried to figure out a way to get me safely from the shore into the raft, I almost hoped they couldn't find a way. *Maybe I'm not up to this,* I thought to myself. *What if the raft tips over? Will I be strong enough to save myself? Will*

I make a fool of myself or ruin everyone else's fun? As my mind continued to race with fears and doubts, Jim Hurst's voice interrupted.

"Hey, we found a spot that isn't as steep!"

Oh, no, I thought, but managed a smile.

With much assistance, my friends helped me down the slope into the river, and pushed my wheelchair out to one of the rafts as it passed by. As our raft raced past the riverbank, I realized there was no turning back. I steadied myself on the raft and tried to focus on the conversation rather than capsizing. For the next six hours my fears were kept at bay, as we drifted down the river and I watched the others swimming alongside the raft. Watching my friends in the water, I longed to join them.

I can either let fear keep me sitting here feeling sorry for myself, or I can try to do as much as I can, I thought to myself.

Taking a deep breath, I fell backwards into the water, similar to a scuba diver falling out of a boat, and began to swim back to the surface and upstream. I re-submerged within a few seconds only to find I was already five feet downstream from the raft. I fought against the current as hard as I could but I was still losing ground. I was in trouble. Luckily, Jim saw me, dove into the river, and surfaced by my side within seconds. With him standing on the bottom and me swimming as hard as I could with my arms, we slowly made headway. Minutes later we successfully made it back to the raft. Jim tried to push me back into it, thinking I had fallen out by accident.

"No, I want to swim to that waterfall with the rest of you," I said.

Knowing he wasn't going to talk me out of it, we headed for

the nearby falls where the others were swimming. Jim continued to swim against the current, pulling me. I found I could reach the bottom with my hands, so I grabbed rocks on the bottom and pulled myself along. Several minutes later, I was with everyone else under the falls. I turned to Jim, "A man can do anything with God's help, the will to do it, and enough friends."

We played for the next half hour under the falls. Later that day one of my friends recounted his view of what had happened: "If you want to sit and give in to your fears, people are willing to let you. On the other hand, if you are in a tough situation and are fighting back, most people are willing to help you. Seeing you overcome your fears gives them hope that they can overcome theirs."

The Fear of Failure

Probably one of the greatest learned fears is the fear of failure. Instead of trying to combat this fear, we often don't try at all. The often subconscious thought, *If I don't try, I can't fail,* corners us into a place of a complacency—even paralysis. Don't let this type of thinking stagnate your growth. Even Thomas Edison admitted that becoming a successful inventor was the result of persistence, not brilliance. He admitted to making hundreds of useless inventions before the useful ones. Remember, if you let fear stop you, it is a choice you are making. While fear is something we all must live with, quitting in response to fear is not! We have a choice about how we react to fear. We can add one more fear to an ever-growing list until we have so many fears that we are locked in a prison of our own making. Or, we can face our fears and trust God with the outcome.

Fear prevented humankind from reaching out to foreign lands for centuries. Stories of sea monsters and giants stopped people from dreaming and superstitions kept civilizations from advancing for eons. Fear has absolutely paralyzed men and women from accomplishing their goals since time began. As in these cases, oftentimes our fears get blown out of proportion and are not nearly as big as we make them out to be in our minds.

Here are a few steps to help you face your fears, both real and imagined:

- Talk to others who have faced similar fears in support groups, church groups, etc.

- Make a list of the things that scare you. You will be amazed at how petty some of your fears really are when you take the time to actually list or describe them. Try writing about your larger fears. Oftentimes just getting them out of your mind and on paper can make you feel better.

- Take small steps against your fears. If you are afraid of something like darkness, then try using smaller or less bright lights in succession until you can sleep in darkness. This works for most of our fears. Take small steps to overcome your fears.

- Fear is an emotion that is beneficial to us—warning us of danger, an intruder, that something is not quite right—unless it is taken to an extreme. In the case of severe phobias, fear can be paralyzing. Seek treatment if you are paralyzed by phobias or anxiety. Thankfully, today there is help for such conditions. Sometimes your fears are well placed. For instance, if you face the fear of an abusive mate, you need to get help and/or remove yourself from the situation until your mate gets help. If the problem persists, speak to your pastor, rabbi, counselor, etc., about other solutions. Fears of violence or abuse are warnings to be heeded, not phobias to be overcome.

- If any of your emotions consistently overshadows the others, then that emotion might be out of control. Seek help to uncover the reasons and to deal with them appropriately.

Step 5

Let Love and Laughter
Get You Through

*Now faith, hope and love abide . . . and the greatest of
these is love.*

—1 Corinthians 13:13

In Sickness and in Health . . .

One of the most depressing memories of my stay in the hospital was the day Milt lost his will to keep trying. Milt was a young man who was transferred to the unit shortly after I arrived. He took no time in telling us that the pretty lady in the photo tacked to his wall was his fiancée. He vowed that he would be standing on his own, waiting to take her hand when they married the next year. Every weekend she would drive up to see him, and the following Monday, I'd notice he had a gleam in his eye, and he would manage an extra dip on the parallel bars.

One Monday he looked sick. He looked whiter than usual, and he sat on the edge of the room and only participated when prodded. One of the men told me that Milt's fiancée hadn't visited this past weekend. The next week, Milt received a letter that she couldn't see him anymore. Week after week, I watched him sink further into despair, until the therapists noted him as "unable to improve to the point of walking on his own."

Milt's was not an isolated event. Wheeling through the halls, I heard many muffled Dear John speeches. I overheard one wife tell her husband, "When I said for better or worse, I didn't mean this." With that, she walked out of his room as nonchalantly as you'd walk out of a restaurant.

It hit me that Wanice could very well be feeling the same thing. She didn't pledge her love and life to a paraplegic. The next time she came to visit, I asked her flat out.

"Wanice, you might be in a situation that you feel obligated to see through. I just want you to know, you don't have to go through it."

"What are you taking about?" she blurted out incredulously.

"I've just got to know. If you feel you can't stick by me . . . if you feel like you can't be my wife, I'll understand. I'm offering you a one-time proposition out, and I really wouldn't blame you."

Tears welled up in her eyes, and her throat caught as she uttered the most beautiful words I had heard in a long time. "Rob, I love you more now than the day I married you. In a strange way, you need me more than you ever have before, and that makes me feel more valuable." She paused, "Besides, you wouldn't leave me if I was in your situation, would you?"

She was right. From then on, the issue was dropped. We had reached "the worse" in our "for better or worse," and we had survived. Yet the challenging times were just beginning as we faced a new life together "on the outside."

With each day we learned that we both had to readjust our relationship and our roles. Any love, whether it's with a spouse, a friend or a relative, will change through the years. It's been said that the three stages of love are from Lust to Rust to Dust. We can prevent our relationships from turning to dust—but it takes work, time, commitment, and a series of constant, tiny readjustments.

I'm extremely independent, and Wanice is very much a "take the reins" type of person. This was always a source of contention between us. However, after my fall I totally relied on her help for several months; she was also caring for two kids who were totally dependent, too. Even though she was in complete control, she wasn't fulfilled. Instead, having to do everything for me and the boys stressed her out—as it would anyone.

Wanice handled everything masterfully for a while: She took care of the boys, paid all of the bills and designed our house to make it fully accessible to my wheelchair. She drew the design on the back of an envelope and a builder built it to her specifications. She made sure all the doors were three feet wide with tile walkways around the carpet so I wouldn't wear it out.

But, with my being able to get around the house more easily and after my second back surgery and stint in rehab, I grew more independent. Wanice had a tough time letting go, and this caused major problems. By the time the boys started school, and I had gotten my career back on track, suddenly Wanice didn't feel needed anymore.

Her whole identity during those years had been as a caretaker for me and the children. (She was a teacher before the boys were born and didn't return to teaching as a substitute until they were older.) At long last, her depression over the accident hit her. She had set it aside on the back burner because she was too busy running our family to deal with her emotions. As problems built up between us, we separated for a brief period. Thanks to counseling, our marriage since then has gotten even better.

I would love to say that our sex life has not suffered, but of course, it has. My injury caused a lack of sensation from the waist down, including sexual organs. While I can still have erections, I cannot feel anything. For me, this is extremely frustrating since I still feel desire, yet no feeling of pleasure. While we make love less often, it is very special when we do.

In a real sense, we had to change our actions over time, everything from chores to our love life. Although there are no perfect love relationships, our marriage has been successful because we made a commitment to stay together, and made adjustments every single day, in both big and small ways. Just as God loves us unconditionally, we must love others the same way—especially spouses. If we love them for what they do for us, this love will fail. Love them for what they are alone.

We still have different ideas about things. I'm kind of a seat-of-the-pants, spontaneous person who can handle just about anything that comes my way when I travel, from a broken axle on my three-wheeled motorcycle to arriving at an airport rental car agency to find my reservation for a hand-controlled vehicle has been lost. Wanice, on the other hand, prefers to go first class all the way. So we compromise. She's always had to hold down the fort when I traveled, whether for work or evangelizing, so I make a point of bringing her home something and making our time together special when I am home. And Wanice will tell you that, when I gave up speaking for a while, it was just too hard for me. It's something I need to do, and now she understands this and continues to encourage me.

And while I thank God every day that Wanice stuck by me, I like to think that I could have survived had her answer been different. I think I could have gone on because I realized something very important—that you are never without love if you love God and believe in yourself.

Although it is sometimes difficult to remember, know that in order to love others and God, you must love yourself.

If you wait to be loved by others before you love them back, you might have a long wait. Your love for others and yourself should have nothing to do with how others love you. Once you love yourself, you will feel good about yourself. Each time you put yourself in a winning frame of mind, it is easier to succeed at your goal. However, each time you put yourself down, it is easier to feel like a loser. You will just be realizing a self-fulfilling prophecy about yourself. You may say, "I am no good, therefore, my life will amount to no good." I firmly believe that in life there are no losers; just those who think they are. You have everything you need to be a productive and successful person, even in the face of adversity. Simply because God loves you, you have worth.

I learned this valuable lesson from my Granny Bryant. For as long as I could remember, Sundays were a great adventure because of my granny and the life lessons we learned in her beloved garden.

❈   ❈   ❈

"Hurry! It's time to go," I screamed with excitement.

"Don't wait on me," my older brother Mike yelled as he passed by me in a rush.

My younger brother Steve was excited, too, but being the youngest, he was the last one to the car. His six-year-old legs were carrying him as fast as possible. The Sunday service was finally over. We patiently waited in line to shake the preacher's hand, and now the magic could finally begin. Dad was taking far too much time unlocking the car. I was about to say something about his lack of speed, but Mom read my thoughts and glared at me to be patient. Finally, the car was unlocked, and we all piled in for our weekly pilgrimage. It was more like an adventure than a mere trip across town. We were going to Granny's house! The anticipation started building early each week. The week slowly passed, and finally it was Sunday afternoon. These were "magical moments," when time stood still.

After saying our hellos, all of us children would meet at the back door with anticipation. We burst through the back door like children running into the living room on Christmas morning. For a moment, we just stood there in the backyard, drinking in the vast array of colors and aromas. We were lost in the immensity of what we saw. It was as if we had just stepped out of Kansas and into Oz.

To the right were huge rows of beautiful flowers of every size and description. The colors defied description and were sprayed with hues that had to be out of the color spectrum. Bees busily carried on their tedious work, and we looked at the perfectly straight rows of carefully tilled dark earth. Behind the flowers were unknown vegetables yet to poke their heads above the ground. To the left was Granny's clothesline. It had vines crawling up the poles, and the branches were laced with various colored vegetables. Then we slowly turned our heads toward "The Garden." To use the word "garden" for the vast radiance that lay before us was a gross understatement.

We all hurried to discover all the living things growing there. At the same time, we understood this was Granny's domain. This was a place in which she took great pride. We knew better than to run onto freshly plowed earth and kill the new growth. We knew we'd be in big trouble if we did this. Of course, our parents would spank us. However, that held no meaning compared to the look of disappointment we would see on Granny's face. She would be hurt if we destroyed something she put such a large part of her life and love into.

We were on holy ground, so to speak, and were there by invitation only. To violate that sacred trust and see Granny's disappointment would be more than we could bear. The older cousins taught the younger ones how to act in Granny's garden. There were occasional infractions, but these were normally followed by punishment by other cousins. We tended to keep these infractions inside our ranks so that we would not risk expulsion by the adults.

In the spring, the garden was full of small green leaves poking out of the earth. We made a game out of guessing which vegetable it was. We discovered who was right by looking at the neatly displayed seed packet tacked onto a small stick at the end of the row. In the summer, the garden took on a whole new appearance as the harvest began. We picked vegetables from the largest watermelon to the tiniest red tomato. They could be eaten raw or picked and given to Granny with great pride. Looking back on it, it was Granny's garden, so we were giving to her what was already hers. She would hug us and thank us just the same, though. This principle helped me understand the idea of tithing our money and time to God. The earth and all its riches are His anyway, but it makes us feel good to give it to Him in a willing manner.

In the fall, the garden changed again into brown colors, and the last harvest was gathered. The winter held no less excitement for us. With great anticipation, we dreamed about the spring and helping Granny once again.

Pass the Pepper, Please

I will always remember the summer I did not heed Granny's warning about one of the vegetables.

"Children, watch how I pick my vegetables. You don't want to hurt the branch or vine. If you do it properly, I will let you pick and eat any of my vegetables. However, there is one vegetable I do not want you to pick or eat. Even if you just touch these and rub your eyes, they can hurt you. These are cherry-red peppers. They will burn your mouth so bad you'll think you're on fire," she warned.

We could see how serious she was and did not dare question such a simple command. Besides, she just might get out her wooden spoon! One Sunday afternoon, my brother Mike and I got into a contest of some sort, trying to prove who was the toughest.

"Oh, yeah, if you're so tough, why don't you eat one of those cherry peppers?" I challenged Mike.

"I will if you will," he returned.

We both stood our ground in this stalemate until Mike made his move toward the garden. I was hot on his heels. We walked boldly through the rows until we came to our final destination. We looked at the little red peppers. They were so small. What harm could possibly come from taking a bite of the little red objects? Besides with the name "cherry," how hot could they be?

We simultaneously picked one and looked at each other with defiance in our eyes. We knew we were saying we were tough enough to eat one and to break the rules to prove it. Now *that* was tough! Mike and I both waited for the other to make the first move. We were beyond the point of no return. The only question was who was going to be first. As if we were speaking telepathically, we realized the one to take the first bite would be the toughest. Suddenly, we both crammed them into our mouths and began munching. *No, that's not good enough,* I thought. I swallowed it also and boldly looked into my brother's eyes. He was glaring back at me and swallowed his with an exaggerated gulp.

"I bit first!" I yelled.

"No, I . . ."

He paused. Slowly the look of defiance that was written on his face changed to one of pain.

He began to turn red, his eyes began to water and he began to choke. I began to laugh, when slowly I felt a burning sensation rise in my mouth. At first, it was like a fireball candy, but it kept growing hotter. Soon it felt as if I had swallowed acid. I opened my mouth and spit out what was left of the pepper. I tried to breathe in cold air to see if it would help. It was worse! Soon our stomachs began to burn. Every internal organ that came in contact with the little pepper began hurting. I didn't want to even imagine the final passage of the cherry-red pepper.

Suddenly, we found ourselves choking and screaming in pain. We ran for the back of the house and we both took turns spraying our mouths out with the garden hose. Mom and Dad came to the back door to see what the commotion was. No words were necessary to tell them what had happened. Granny fixed a concoction of bread and strange-tasting condiments. It was not a quick cure, however, and our mouths continued to burn for hours. The worst part, though, was looking into Granny's eyes and seeing disappointment. It was not a concocted face;

it was the look of genuine pain she felt because we had not listened to her. She never said a word, but that look taught us a valuable lesson.

Garden Lessons

There were other dangers in the garden also. Several times, one of us was startled as a snake crawled by or curled up and flicked its tongue at us. If one of the girls saw it first, the real danger was deafness as they shrieked like an F-16 jet. Normally, these snakes were harmless, but occasionally a copperhead would raise its ugly head. Granny explained how important the balance in nature was, and how all the animals played a role.

"You see, the snakes eat the little critters that eat my garden. Even though they are ugly and scary looking, their role in life is no less important than any other creature's. Take this worm, for example," she said as she lifted an earthworm from a freshly plowed furrow. Of course, several girls screamed at the ugly crawling thing, and this was a signal to the boys as to which girl could be scared later by putting an earthworm down the back of her shirt. Granny would clear her throat to regain our attention.

"You see, this worm crawls through my garden, and it makes holes wherever it goes. These holes allow the oxygen to get to the roots of my plants, and the plants grow stronger. Everything has its place and has importance in the overall scheme of things."

She never said it, but we knew we were like the animals and

insects in her garden. We were all different, yet no more or less important than the other grandchildren in her eyes. Like God's unconditional love, she loved us all just for who we were. When I entered Granny's garden, I knew I was loved. Not because I was special in any way, just simply because I was me.

You, too, are special because God made you just the way you are! You are unique and have special talents and abilities that no one else has. God has a mission for your life that is unique also. You are created in God's own image. What more could you possibly need in order to feel loved and feel good about yourself?

Everything is funny as long as it is happening to somebody else.

—*Will Rogers*

In Order to Heal, Laugh Until It Hurts

Just as important as love is in life, so is laughter. There is a time for tears. All of us have times in our life when we are down. If you just learned that you had a disease, you would be abnormal if you weren't sad. In fact, you would probably go through a whole gamut of emotions. This is to be expected. Give yourself time to heal. Men, we need to cry and allow our emotions to flow as well. Don't bottle them up; one day you will explode. However, if tears or sorrow have become a way of life, this chapter is for you. A good healthy laugh will help heal your wounds.

Maintaining a sense of humor is absolutely essential to your health. Laugh at yourself; have fun. Life is too short to be so serious that you can't see the humor in things. The Bible tells us: "To everything, there is a season . . . a time to weep, and a time to laugh" (Ecclesiastes 3:1,4). In my opinion, more people are defeated by the inability to find humor in things than by anything else. I have known people who go through entire days without a single laugh. To me, this is inconceivable! If your life is so serious that you can't laugh, you are defeated! Often the inability to laugh is caused by deep feelings and painful emotions, which in turn were caused by hardship or tragedy. If this is the case with you, I strongly suggest that you consult with a counselor. There are also medical conditions that require a physician's care. Chronic and deep depression, some eating disorders, certain mental disorders and chemical imbalances fall into this category. Don't be the "tough" guy or woman who will not seek medical or professional help when it is needed. If you can't laugh, you need help. I'm not saying that you will never be sad or need to cry, but if it is a lifestyle, your lack of humor will greatly affect your health and happiness. As you'll read, a healthy dose of laughter can even get a woman through labor!

Laughter on Delivery

As is typical with firstborn children, our son, Jason, was born at the worst possible time. Or maybe it just seems that way because you have absolutely no idea what to expect. I had just worked sixteen straight hours managing a 7-Eleven. When I got home, I lay down, exhausted, hoping to sleep for at least half a day. Then an hour later, Wanice uttered those terrifying words, "It's time!"

I bolted out of bed, rushed her to the hospital and into a labor room. I was in such a rush that I didn't even go to the bathroom after waking up. My need to urinate seemed so insignificant compared to Wanice's predicament. My wife was now screaming in agony with each contraction. It was my job to coach her through the pains. It was also my job to listen to her yell "You did this to me!" into my left ear.

After an hour, the contractions were less than two minutes apart. She was having her problems, and I was having mine. Now, two hours later, I *really* had to use the bathroom!

There were two bathrooms. One was in our labor room and was shared with the adjoining room. The other one was way down the hall. Just then a nurse walked in. She was a large woman with squinty eyes who looked more like a drill sergeant than a kind caregiver. She looked me up and down as if she was inspecting the shine on my boots. By the look on her face, I knew I had failed inspection! She even sounded like a drill sergeant as she asked, "How far apart are the contractions?"

"They are approximately two minutes apart, and that's my problem."

"Problem? Why is your wife's pain *your* problem?"

I thought her callousness was a little out of place, but I was in her domain, so I let the sarcasm pass.

"Well, you see, I have to 'take care of things.' The closest bathroom is too far down the hall to make it back for her next contraction. Can I use the bathroom that is shared with the next labor room?"

"Absolutely not! No! That is for *mothers* only! Do you understand me?" she screamed at me.

"Yes, sir! I mean 'ma'am,'" I replied out of habit from the military. I could have sworn she was related to a Green Beret soldier I once met.

She left in a huff, as Wanice started her next contraction.

I waited until it was over and then rushed toward the door.

"Where are you going?" Wanice asked with a horrified look on her face.

"I really have to 'take care of things.' Right now!"

"You can't leave me! Just use the bathroom here."

Now I was in a fix. Nurse Green Beret told me not to use this bathroom. Wanice was having our baby and needed me, though. She was the woman I was going to live the rest of my life with. If I ran out now, she would always remember I left her side during contractions. Was I going to listen to a nurse or my wife? I thought about it for one brief, agonizing moment. Wanice was shocked I even had to think about it. She looked at me as if to say, "I can't believe you are going to listen to a total stranger over me." It's amazing what a woman can say with her eyes. Especially a pregnant one!

I dashed into the bathroom. As I said, it was connected to the other labor room so I made sure the other door was closed. However, there was no lock. I began "taking care of things" when suddenly the door to the other room swung wide open. There stood Nurse Green Beret. Her arms were crossed and she was scowling at me with a "drop dead" look on her face. There was no way I could stop in the middle of what I was doing. I stood there and just ignored her and looked at the walls as if I had discovered an interesting pattern in the wallpaper. This only served to make her more angry.

"You stop that and get out of there!" she demanded, realizing how ridiculous the order was, but she could not back down now. I, of course, could not stop midstream (so to speak) either, especially after having put it off for so long, so we had a standoff on our hands.

To make matters worse, the pregnant woman in the next room had a full view of my predicament. She was between contractions and began laughing. At first her laughter was soft, but soon she was slapping her sides in laughter. She even laughed sporadically through the next couple of contractions. As a matter of fact, she was not as dilated as Wanice, but she had her baby first. Jason was born several hours later by cesarean section because Wanice had complications. I tried forgetting about my embarrassment and just concentrated on being there for Wanice. However, try as I might, I could not seem to avoid the pregnant lady in the next room or Nurse Green Beret, both of whom had seen my embarrassing predicament. Every time I rounded the corner, there they would be.   ·

As a matter of fact, the other mother thanked me several times for making her delivery easier. She had plenty of time to do that, because she requested to have my wife as her roommate in the post-delivery room. Every time she had visitors, she delightedly told the story again. This excruciatingly embarrassing episode began to feel like the story of my life. But you know what? You may as well get used to laughing at yourself. Chances are, everybody else has at one point or another!

A good sense of humor is not the ability to tell a joke, just the ability to recognize one. Some of us can tell jokes, and some of us can't. But we all need a sense of humor to survive hard times. If you have the ability to laugh at yourself, you'll feel better and your friends will also appreciate you more. One reason we can't laugh at ourselves is we feel inferior in some way. We feel by laughing at ourselves or allowing others to do the same, we are being made a fool. The reality of the situation is that only a foolish person cannot laugh at himself or herself. Don't take yourself so seriously. A good laugh can change your whole outlook for the day. If there are memories that cause you pain and rob you of your ability to laugh, then work your way through them with a good friend who will listen. If the memories persist, unless they are causing other problems in your life, leave them behind and think of memories that bring you happiness. This is not suppression; it is healthy. Why dwell on something that brings you pain? Don't do this to yourself.

Humor can also defuse anger, something very important for people who tend to harbor hostile feelings. Hostility is a major factor in stressful situations, especially if you are the sort of person who stews in his or her own anger or perceived hurt feelings for any period of time. Doctors have shown that this increases blood pressure, aggravates heart disease and produces excess adrenaline and stress chemicals (such as the hormone cortisol). Feeling angry or stressed over things that are absolutely out of your control is not only senseless and a waste of energy, it is unhealthy. You need to learn to "Let go and let God" when your frustration levels soar. Go with the flow! Convert a cynical or snide or insulting or angry attitude into a positive one through humor. If you knew it was your last day on Earth, would you spend it stewing over a traffic jam, your child's torn-apart room or that pile of bills that didn't get mailed on time? I don't think so. If you wake up to face a tough morning, or maybe you got very little sleep, skip the front page of the newspaper and go right to the comics. It can improve your outlook.

Another Embarrassing Episode

Don't get me wrong, I'm not fixated on this area. But since my accident and paralysis, I have to handle bathroom functions differently from most people. It just so happened that one day in church I didn't follow the standard parental advice we give our kids: "Go before you leave home!" The result was I was in desperate straits in the middle of the service—and Wanice thought it was the funniest thing in the world.

There are a lot of complications of paraplegia besides the fact that I can't walk without the aid of braces and crutches. One of those complications is that I have to wear an external catheter and leg bag. I have very little trouble with this aspect of my life as long as I "take care of things" before going on a long trip, to a long party or . . . long church service! I heard one pregnant woman say her greatest fear was breaking her water in public. Well, as you might imagine, I have similar fears all the time.

If I had taken my own advice given to my children before going to church, I would have been okay. But I did not. I also would have been okay if I had stayed in my wheelchair, but I did not do this either. I walked with the aid of my braces and crutches to the middle of the pew. Minutes later, I was in the middle of a pew, blocked in on both sides, in the third row from the front of our very large church. It was along about the seventh verse of a hymn—one in which it seemed like every other word was about water—that I knew I was in deep water, pardon the pun.

The sermon had not even started, and our visiting pastor tended to be long-winded. I contemplated my situation. If I tried to make it to my wheelchair, my catheter would explode. If I waited, I would have the same problem. I felt I had but one recourse. This would involve a complicated maneuver and expert timing and the aid of my beautiful wife. Along about what seemed to be the eighth verse, I couldn't wait any longer. I yanked on the bottom of Wanice's sweater and she sat down beside me to see what I had to say. I told her my situation and instead of getting angry with me, she laughed out loud.

"Well, what can I do about it?"

I told her what she was going to have to do. She stopped laughing and grew pale.

"Here? You want me to go get it right . . ." Just then the hymn ended and my wife was still yelling in the suddenly quiet church, "Now?"

The only thing that saved her was everybody else was standing up and could not see who was yelling "Now?" up in front.

However, the more she thought about it, the more tickled she became. As the next series of hymns began, Wanice grabbed her purse and slid past our neighbors. Once out of the pew, she disappeared from my view past all of the standing congregation. It seemed like an eternity, but she reappeared in a few minutes with a bulging purse. I'm sure no one else noticed, but to me it looked like she was trying to conceal gold from Fort Knox inside that handbag.

Just when I thought my problems were almost over, the congregation finished singing and sat down. I was seemingly "finished" also. What I needed was more singing and organ playing in order to perform our next stunt. I knew if the preaching began, I was in trouble. I said a little prayer and, miraculously, it was answered in the very next moment as our music director stood and walked to the platform.

"We haven't done this for a long time. Are there any requests for your favorite hymn? We will sing the first verse only. Let's take three hymns!"

The congregation remained seated as the first song started. Wanice set her purse down on the floor beside my feet, reached inside and pulled out a very large urinal and I emptied my leg bag into it.

The challenging part now was to get out of the church without displaying the urinal like a trophy. Now this is love! Wanice calmly put it back in her purse and carefully balanced it for the rest of the service. At the conclusion of the service, she carried it out under her arm. The amazing part is she giggled all the way! Since then, I have learned to be better prepared for the unexpected, and to fully appreciate Wanice's ability to find the humor even in the midst of a sticky situation.

Choose Laughter

Sometimes you may as well laugh, otherwise you'll just cry. I travel all over with my job and also witnessing for Christ and speaking. In February 2000, after working all day at my job in Texas, I flew to Los Angeles, stopping on the way in Las Vegas, to speak at Pepperdine University in Malibu the next day. I arrived at midnight, only to find that my reservations to be picked up by a limo service had been canceled due to my late arrival. After we got that straightened out, they took me to West Lake Village Inn in Agoura Hills. I rolled into the lobby at about 1:15 A.M. to discover that, not only couldn't they find my name in the computer, there were no handicap-accessible rooms available.

Finally the night manager asked me to follow him. We headed through the beautiful sprawling landscape between palatial buildings at this very quiet hour. I rolled passed rock atriums with hanging vines draped over trellises. We passed manicured lawns beside duck ponds, babbling brooks, incredible trees and fountains of every size and description. The lights were so spectacular I thought I was back in Vegas. I began wondering where we were going after I had to get out of the chair and climb some stairs with my crutches, but he assured me we were headed in the right direction.

Suddenly, the manager stopped, looked again at the room key in his hands, and got the sickest look on his face. He turned to me and said, "Mr. Bryant, I am *so* sorry—this room is on the second floor!"

Instead of getting angry at the inconvenience and wild goose chase, I just started laughing. He was shocked but smiled in relief that I wasn't mad that he had taken me so far in the wrong direction and up stairs so late at night. We went back down the stairs, back to the office, and then he led me literally two doors down the hall to the correct room. Now this struck me extra funny, that my room was this close to begin with and we had taken the "scenic" route to nowhere, just to end up virtually back where we started from.

He probably thought I was nuts because I was laughing at this misadventure, but I was able to share with him that the reason I can maintain a sense of humor is that Christ gives me joy, and that minor inconveniences cannot steal my joy.

Some of the most miserable people I've ever met have lost their ability to laugh. I know life can be hard and downright cruel sometimes, but you've lost the battle when you've lost your laugh. One of the best ways to defeat adversity is the ability to laugh. For some of us, laughing is easy. For others it is more difficult, but we all need to maintain a sense of humor in order to overcome our adversity.

Here are a few steps to help you flex your humor muscle:

- Try to see the funny part of every situation. Often when people are involved in horrible situations, they tell morbid jokes and find themselves laughing at hardship. Don't be hard on yourself for doing this. This is healthy and will help you deal with the situation. For instance, my uncle and I were having a hard time dealing with my stepfather's death. He came walking out of the bathroom with a smile on his face. I asked him what was funny. He said the name of the soap in the bathroom was, "When the party is over." We had a healthy laugh for hours.

- Read a book of jokes. Send others funny e-mails or subscribe to a "Joke of the Day" e-mail club.

- Be around people who make you laugh. Avoid people or situations that make you sad. This is a no-brainer, but I see this all of the time. Some folks choose to dwell on things or memories that bring them pain. Move on, or don't think about them. Once you work through the tough aspects of life, don't dwell on them. Move on. This is not suppression; this is essential to your health.

- Go to a comedy club or rent a funny movie.

- Give yourself time after tragedy to heal, but then force yourself to do something fun or something that will make you laugh. At first this will be an act of volition, but soon you will be laughing again.

- Finally, if you suffer from a chemical or mental disorder that depresses your emotions, get professional help. If you love yourself and family, you owe it to yourself and them to get well, and laugh again!

Here are a few ways to love yourself in spite of your problems:

- If you have problems loving yourself, talk to a pastor who can explain God's love for you so that you can begin taking small steps toward loving yourself. Next, make a list of all your good attributes and ask friends the things they love about you. You will be amazed at how special you are and why you should love yourself.

- If you have problems loving others, this is normally for the same reason. You cannot love others unless you first love yourself. I suggest you follow the same steps in the bullet above. Then take the risk of loving others. Ninety-nine percent of the time, they will love you right back in a wholesome manner.

- Surround yourself with people who love you. If you are in a home with parents who do not express love easily, then join a church or a church youth group and surround yourself with people who will love you.

- If you are in a marriage with a partner who has trouble expressing love, then I suggest you try counseling. Surround yourself with friends who love you. Many of us have fallen victim to extramarital affairs when we and our mate are not getting along.

- Remember . . . love will get you through.

Step 6

Be a
Good Example

Setting an example is not the main means of influencing another; it is the only means.

—*Albert Einstein*

A ctions really do speak louder than words, which is why setting a good example for others to follow is extremely important. Conversely, if you're experiencing a problem, you should seek out someone who's been there who can act as an example to you. That's my mission with this book: to serve as an example that, with faith, prayer, determination to succeed and hard work, anyone can beat adversity.

Dad, I Remembered

A couple of years ago, a pastor asked me to speak at a camp in Colorado. Upon receiving the itinerary, I began wondering why he wanted me to go. On Monday, the young people were going to rappel down a cliff. Rappelling is a sport that definitely requires strong, healthy legs. A rope is slung through a metal apparatus called a "belay." The rappeller then jumps down a cliff, keeping his or her body perpendicular to the rock face while feeding rope through the belay as fast as he or she feels comfortable. On Tuesday, the young people were going rock climbing. Once again, this requires a great deal of leg strength. On Wednesday, they were going white water rafting, and on Thursday, they were going to hike up a mountain. The trail for mountaineering began at eight thousand feet and culminated in a panoramic view of the valley from an eleven-thousand-foot peak. Obviously, this was not a paraplegic event either, so I called him back on the following week and said, "Hello, Art, this is Rob Bryant. I received your packet about camp and I'm a little confused. I can't do any of the events on the schedule. What exactly do you want me to do?"

"Rob, I am familiar with your limitations. All I want you to do is to speak to the youth each evening after they return from the mountains."

"Oh, okay," I said as I thought about how much fun it would be to go to the mountains. The more I thought about it, the more I liked the idea. I was already going to be away from home several weeks that summer, however, and I missed spending time with my own kids. After another moment of thought, I said, "I will be your camp speaker if you let my sixth-grader Jason come with me. I know that the camp is for junior and senior high school students, but he is probably as tall and strong as any of your junior high kids."

Art said Jason could come, so Jason and I worked out so we would be in quasi-good shape. I was hoping to push my wheelchair through some of the terrain and walk using my braces and crutches up small hills. The months passed, and soon Jason and I found ourselves on one of three buses headed to Colorado. It began like any other youth trip, with one crisis after another. First one of the buses broke down, several air conditioners broke down, and almost all of the counselors broke down just on the way to the mountains. So instead of arriving at 9:00 P.M., we arrived at 1:00 A.M. We were exhausted and needed to stretch out when we finally were permitted to leave the confines of our bus seats. Sleep was not difficult. On the following morning after breakfast, the buses took the kids out to the rappelling and climbing site. I couldn't go, of course, so I stayed in my room and began preparing for my message that night. But while I was studying, I heard a voice in my heart say, *Rob, run the race.*

I had not heard that voice since I began training for The Miracle Walk.

What race? I thought. I can't do any of the daily events. What was this nagging feeling asking me to do? I thought perhaps it meant I should go to the mountain and watch the kids and encourage them. I found two leaders, Kim Whirt and Mark Roberts, who were heading that way, so I bummed a ride.

I was amazed at what I saw when we got there. The rappelling site was an 80-foot cliff, on the side of a 250-foot hill, on top of a mountain. I am a little afraid of heights considering my history that landed me in the wheelchair. I stood using my braces and watched the young people. Jason looked down and saw me standing below and waved excitedly. Suddenly, once again I heard the voice in my heart, *Rob, run the race.*

I looked at the side of the hill in front of me. There was no trail for my wheelchair and it was much too steep for me to walk up using my braces. The only way that I could attempt to proceed was to crawl. *This was ridiculous!* I thought. I couldn't possibly crawl all the way up there. There were rocks, ledges and steep dirt embankments. But I could not shake the feeling that I was being called to join my son and the other young people at the top of the cliff.

"Mark, I've got to try this. Would you help me?"

He stood there looking at me as if he had not heard my words properly. He was not sure of what to say, so he blurted out, "Sure, I'll help."

I walked as far as I could with my crutches and braces before falling on my face. Then I began to crawl. Several of the youth saw what was happening below and began to encourage us. It was very difficult, but with Mark and Kim's help, we began making headway. I was embarrassed because I had to crawl like a baby, but it was the only thing I could do on that terrain. Mark helped by pulling on my shoulders while Kim would either push from behind or block my feet with hers to give me an occasional rest. Within an hour, we were over halfway up, and we rested. Many of the young people joined us on our ascent. I watched Jason as he rappelled down the rock face. He passed by me on his way back up and smiled at me, but he had a worried look in his eye. Within another hour we made it to the top. The kids cheered as they saw us.

While resting on a rock, I realized why Jason had a concerned look on his face. I looked down over the cliff and suddenly realized I was going to have to crawl back down the hill the same way I had come. My hands and knees were already bleeding, and I was exhausted. Then a thought came to me. I watched the young people rappel for a while and realized that if I was strong enough to push my body off of the rocks with one arm, I could use the other arm to hold onto the rope. It was safe, right? (Of course, I thought the derrick was safe the day I fell off of that, too!) My mind was suddenly filled with memories of my accident, and fear made its way into every thought. I fought the fear back and crawled over to the line of young people. After a few minutes it was my turn. The counselor looked at me with curiosity.

"Are you going to rappel?" Arlo Guthrie (no relation) asked, not trying to sound like he doubted I could.

"I think it would be easier to let myself down by rope rather than crawl back down off of this mountain."

He thought about it for a second and said, "Yeah, I believe you have a point there."

He explained the various ropes to me, hooked me into a harness, put a helmet on me and yelled down below to the anchorman, Drew Pickle.

"Rob is coming down. Get ready to jam on the brakes if he needs you."

What this meant was that the rope ran to the ground below. By simply pulling down on the bottom of the rope, the rope tightened inside the belay and stopped all forward movement.

I knew better than to think about it for any length of time, you know, "Feel the fear and do it anyway," so I quickly rolled over to the side of the cliff and went over the edge sideways. I was on my way, and there was no turning back! The rope pulled on the harness, and I whipped around so that my feet were down. I tried using my legs to stand perpendicular on the rock face, but I kept falling to the side and beating my shoulders against the rocks. Then I began pushing off of the rock with my left arm and began letting rope out with my right. This worked better, but it was very difficult. My arms were already exhausted from the crawl up the hill. I rested for a second and decided I was going too slowly. My tired arms could not stand very much more. I began letting the rope out faster, and soon I was moving rather quickly. The only problem was that I was rubbing my body against the rock face so hard, the rocks were actually ripping my skin. Soon my shirt was torn and my arms were scraped, but I didn't care, I was rappelling!

Drew (the anchorman) was ready in case I started moving too quickly. He never had to help. Soon I was sitting on the ground. Cheers erupted all around and Jason gave me a hug. I didn't think about it at the time, but this was a brave move for

Jason. He was the youngest person on the mountain that day, and I'm sure he wanted them to think he was just as mature as they were. Normally this does not include hugging a parent. But he told me he was proud of me loud enough for the others to hear. I made my way back to the bus on my braces with a lot of help from the kids. You could have heard a pin drop on the bus as I began sharing my testimony with them. Many of the kids told me they would never quit again!

After dinner, I spoke to a tired yet receptive group of kids who knew I had paid the price and I earned their respect. On day two, we went rock climbing, and I failed miserably. I only went twenty feet up a cliff. The kids were going at least fifty. But an amazing thing happened. Several of the young people were not going to try. But after I tried, they lined up and said, "Do me next."

Wednesday was rafting, and this was not difficult for me since I had worked my upper arms since the accident. At the halfway point, they portaged (carried the rafts) up on a beach and rested. Several of the stronger ones carried me with them. It was not easy for them. It was also not easy for me. It was a reminder that I was disabled, and I needed to do what I could and not worry about the things I couldn't do.

On Thursday morning, the alarm sounded and the young people took the bus to the mountaineering trail. I was very relieved on this day when I did not hear a voice in my heart to "Run the race." I watched Jason as he loaded up with the rest of the kids. Just before he got on he said, "Dad, when I am mountaineering, I'll climb the mountain for you. I know you want to but can't. Dad, I promise to do my best, just like you would if you could."

I looked away from him as tears got the best of me. I

remembered another time when Jason was being interviewed on TV. He told the interviewer that when he ran, he ran as fast as he could because he knew I would if I could, and he felt like he was running for the two of us.

I was so proud of him as he climbed onto the bus. Later that day I heard the story over and over from the other junior high students who were with Jason on the mountain trail. Jason was the youngest student that day, but he knew he had to do his best. When he was near the top he actually began running. Most of the other kids were ill with altitude sickness, or so tired they could barely stand, much less run. A few of them tried to catch him, but couldn't. I asked him later what he was thinking about when he began to run up the mountain. Jason is a man of few words, but he said, "Dad, I remembered."

"Remembered what?" I asked.

I had to press him pretty hard, but he indicated that he remembered when I walked from Fort Worth to Dallas on braces and crutches, as well as several other things he watched me do that I had long since forgotten.

Giving Her Best

In 1998, I was training by powering a hand-cycle in a one-hundred-mile bike race in Wichita Falls fondly called "The Hotter than Hell 100." There were eighty-two hundred able-bodied participants, and I actually beat twenty-five hundred riders by riding nonstop. I did not stop at any rest stops so that I could keep up with the much faster bikes. My friends on the bikes saw what I was doing and brought me water and fruit so that I didn't have to stop. It was exhausting, but it was the only way for me to compete. It took me just over eight hours of continuous pedaling with my arms. The Wichita Falls newspaper wrote a marvelous article about me and Jonathan, who was riding with me. The local CBS affiliate covered my ride before, during and after. I had no idea I could go that far without stopping.

Soon after, I was raising money for the Multiple Sclerosis Society by riding with two hundred other bike riders on a 150-mile trip. It was a two-day ride through the hills of five counties south of Fort Worth. I was the only paraplegic, so everyone else was riding normal eighteen-speed bikes while I was riding my hand-cycle. Some of the hills were very large and the temperature was in the upper nineties. I made many new friends and have pictures that I will cherish for a lifetime. NBC followed me for thirty miles on the first day, and I was delighted to see a five-minute spot on the 6:00 P.M., 10:00 P.M. and 8:00 A.M. news reports. Amazingly, I actually came in within the top third of the riders who were using bikes and legs. It made me realize that if we push ourselves just a little bit harder, anything is possible. Besides, if we don't, our competition will.

But by far the most rewarding moment came after the race when a woman with multiple sclerosis (MS) asked to speak with me. She had been riding on the back of a motorcycle both days so we developed a friendship. My only regret is that I never got her whole name. Many riders were standing with me as we were celebrating and dancing to some loud music. Most of us had a tremendous amount of respect for her ability to face MS with such courage, so as she began speaking riders walked over closer to hear her faint voice.

"Rob, you have encouraged me to face another day when I

saw you struggling along mile after mile, hill after hill, and refusing to give up. As you know, I, too, face hardship. As a matter of fact, one of my biggest struggles is against the heat and sun. They can completely sap me of my waning strength."

She paused and her husband, who was standing behind her, began weeping. He knew what she was about to do. She calmly reached up and took off her bonnet that was protecting her from the heat. Then she gave it to me, saying, "You've given me so much today that I want you to have this."

Mere words could never describe how I felt at that moment. Fifty riders who were looking on were moved as well. No one could say anything. We all hugged each other and left knowing we would never forget her or her words. The bonnet is on my desk at work now, and I pull it out whenever I am facing a challenge. Her courage and sacrifice will spur me on for years. She understood that the best way to overcome her potential bitterness because of her struggle with MS was giving to others. I will never forget her! She has overcome her adversity more than most folks that have no physical problems at all.

When you encourage others, you will receive the biggest blessing. You will receive the thankfulness and admiration of others. Someday, all things come back to us—good *and* bad!

Management 101

I came to the conclusion that others will do as we do. They will try their best if they see us trying our best. Success or failure is not nearly as important as trying our best. I succeeded at rappelling and seemingly failed at rock climbing.

Oftentimes what we see as failure, those around us see as success. We are successful if we encourage those around us to try their best, even though we may feel we failed in a specific task. The common denominator, which both of my sons remember, is "trying." Your family (especially children) will remember your words and your deeds. They will remember the good things you've done as well as the bad.

By setting a good example, you in turn will motivate others to help you. I recently worked ten straight fourteen-hour days in Charleston, South Carolina, on the Army Pre-Position Ships contract that needed help from a variety of experts on several different subjects. DynCorp sent quality control inspectors, mechanics and administrators from all over to assist. It was exhausting, but rewarding since we were able to make great improvements in the maintenance of tanks, trucks and vehicles for the U.S. Army. (We inherited the problem when we took over this job from a competitor.) Every day management held a breakfast meeting at our hotel, then we worked from 7 A.M. to 7 P.M., after which we closed the day with a meeting as well.

The military base is rather small so I didn't rent a car, just rolled my wheelchair for miles each day from building to building. One day I was talking with a tank driver who was working unbelievably hard and asked him how he did it. I was surprised at his answer.

"Mr. Bryant, I have been watching you out here with us pushing your wheelchair all over this place, and I told myself that if you could do it, so could I," he said. "Here you are, a big shot from corporate headquarters, and you don't mind getting dirty out here with the rest of us."

Several of the guys standing around us said similar things

and I was thrilled that I had encouraged them just by working as hard as I could.

One day while rolling through one of the offices I saw a young man who was very discouraged about something. When I asked him what was wrong, he said, "Mr. Bryant, I have been here for three weeks and my paycheck got lost. My wife is here and I can't even take her out to eat. Could you help me by calling headquarters and seeing where my paycheck is?" Of course I called and was told that they would Fed Ex his paycheck to him the next day. Then I opened my wallet and handed him fifty dollars (all I had with me at the time) to hold him over until his check arrived. He was dumbfounded that I gave him my own money. Word got around about what I had done and I'm convinced these people worked even harder. You don't need an MBA to be a great leader, just follow the advice given in the Sermon on the Mount. After all, Christ taught Management 101 over two thousand years ago, and he led His own great team—His disciples.

A Child Shall Lead Them

One of the most inspirational leaders I ever knew was a youngster who provided a very dramatic example to people of all ages on how to conduct one's life—and death. There was a very normal, healthy boy at our church by the name of Lynn. Then, when he was about ten years old, Lynn was diagnosed with a terminal illness. Within months, he was diagnosed with a second terminal illness that was totally unrelated to the first one! Jerry, Lynn's dad, was my Sunday school teacher at the time. We watched the family as Lynn became sicker and moved from health to braces, and eventually a wheelchair. This was long before my own injury, so I knew little of what disabled people go through. We watched Lynn and Jerry as they faced this difficult time with the utmost courage. One day I asked Jerry a question.

"Jerry, I know you and Lynn used to play Follow the Leader. I don't mean to be insensitive in any way, but how do you play Follow the Leader now?"

"Well, at first, when Lynn was on braces and crutches, I would walk very slowly in front of him and say, 'Follow me.' You see, we just simply began calling our game Follow Me. Then after Lynn was in a wheelchair, I rented another chair and I would roll along the sidewalk in front of him and say, 'Follow me, Son.' Sometimes Lynn would be the leader and roll in front of me and say, 'Follow me, Dad.'"

As the months passed, Lynn grew much worse. Soon he could not move his arms either. I hesitated to pry into their suffering, but Jerry was always eager to talk about his son.

"Jerry, once again, I don't mean to be insensitive in any way, but how do you play Follow Me now?"

"It is more difficult, but one way we play is at suppertime, when it's tough for him to eat. I will put a fork under my food and raise it to my mouth and say, 'Follow me, Son.'"

A few months later, Lynn was baptized. Lynn was very afraid of deep water since he could not move his arms or legs. There was little chance of the pastor dropping him into the deep water, but everyone understood why he was anxious. Lynn asked if his dad could help and be baptized at the same time. Of course the pastor agreed. After Jerry was baptized, Lynn played Follow Me and went next. There was not a dry eye in the church when Lynn asked the pastor if he could say a few words. The pastor just nodded at the boy; he was so moved he couldn't speak.

"Many of you out there feel sorry for me," he said. "Don't! Very soon, I'll be in a better place where I'll run with two healthy legs. As a matter of fact, while you are testing out your wings, look down, I'll be the one running."

Within a year, Lynn was on his deathbed. Lynn could barely speak and asked his dad to bring his ear down to his mouth. Some of Lynn's last words were, "Dad, I'm leaving now to see Jesus . . . follow me."

Lynn was an example for many of us, and we have been following him ever since. Where we lead, others will follow! I look forward to racing against him in heaven someday. Remember, people are not watching us when times are easy. Anyone can do well then. They watch us when times are hard because that is when we are really ourselves. Be an example! It will bless you and your family all the days of your life. Someone is following your example; someone is right behind you. Where are you going? And who is following your lead?

Step 7

Ask for Help

No man is an island.

—John Donne

United We Stand

No matter how much we may want to take all the credit for some great feat, chances are we weren't alone in our accomplishment. It took a team of therapists and nurses and aides to get me walking again, and another team to help me walk over twenty-four miles from one Texas city to another, and several teams to enable me to row across the U.S. in my RowCycle, which you'll read about in chapter 9 in part III. And I wouldn't have accomplished any of this without the help of family and friends.

Any good manager, coach, military leader, teacher or administrator knows, that if the people under him or her aren't united in a common effort as a team, you've got a problem on your hands. You may have the best and brightest people working for you, but if it's every man or woman for him- or herself, or if they're all working at cross-purposes, you'll fail.

The story I am about to relate occurred years ago and serves to illustrate the point that we need to rely on teamwork to make it. I learned this while on vacation in the "hill country" of Southwest Texas.

Enchanted Rock

"There it is up ahead," our driver, Rock, said with excitement. The six sets of eyes were anxiously glued to the windows looking at the skyline ahead for any signs of our destination. Our first glimpse of it vanished after we went around another curve. Deep in the hill country of Southwest Texas near Austin, we topped the next hill and a grand view filled the horizon. As far as our eyes could see there were rolling hills, green trees and brown rock. Right in the center of this feast for the eyes was Enchanted Rock. It is one of the largest outcroppings of pure granite in the nation. Standing fourteen hundred feet above the surrounding Texas floor, it looked like a domed mosque of pure marble. It was composed of earth-tone shades of brown with pink and lighter shades of granite, giving it a striking appearance as it emerged from the ground; it literally resembled a giant bald head.

There were six of us in the van on a well-deserved weekend getaway. All of us were escaping our own individual rat races. Rock and Sandra Shoemaker had a daughter and worked as an engineer and an administrator, respectively. Mike and Julie Brantley had a set of twins, a newborn, and worked as an attorney and homemaker. Mike could not even get away from the phone for the weekend. His cellular phone was constantly ringing in efforts of scheduling a trial on the following Monday. My wife and I longed for a weekend without work or speaking engagements. For us, this was it—a real live vacation!

That morning we ate a tightly scheduled breakfast and had a quick shopping tour. Now my friends had just enough time to climb Enchanted Rock before racing to a local museum that

Mike and Rock wanted to see. Our weekend was relaxing only because we were away from our regular routines. We were still running around like chickens with their heads cut off. But we were away from kids, bosses and other stresses. We were all having a marvelous time until. . . .

We pulled into the parking lot beside the ranger station, paid our fee and proceeded toward Enchanted Rock. We parked as close as possible to the huge igneous intrusion. After we stopped, Mike and Rock pulled out my wheelchair. After crossing a smooth parking lot surface, we arrived at a small pavilion that had a map of the various hiking trails leading to the very top of Enchanted Rock.

I was as strong as an ox with braces and crutches, and could possibly have slowly walked to the top. Fate had other plans however, because one week prior, I had burned my right heel on a very hot boat engine. It was a bad second-degree burn that went all the way to the muscle. My doctor took my braces away for four months knowing that, if they were still on, I might walk on the heel regardless since I can't feel pain.

We stopped for a moment at the bottom of the hill to take pictures, and I wished them a good time. So there I sat as my friends began walking up Enchanted Rock. Before leaving, Sandra gave me the keys to the van, just in case I grew thirsty. I was also supplied with the Brantleys' binoculars. I put them in my wheelchair backpack before grabbing a book to read.

I was moderately content to let my friends do the climbing while I sat there. There wasn't anything I could do about it, anyway, so what was the point? Enchanted Rock was not close to being wheelchair accessible, and with the burn, I was wheelchair-bound. The Americans with Disabilities Act has done great things; however, it has not made all mountains wheelchair accessible. I could have asked my friends to help me go a short distance, but I knew I would drastically slow them down and usually I try not to impose upon my friends. I would have few friends if I threw a pity party for myself and asked them to do everything for me. Besides, they were not even physically capable of helping me. Rock was in great shape, but I outweighed him by fifty pounds. Mike was larger than I was, but he had bad knees from his college football days.

Rolling to the Top

Resigning myself to the fact I was not going anywhere, I began reading my book. But every once in a while I would cast a hungry look toward the mountain in front of me. That's when the hero of the story entered the picture.

"I noticed your friends are hiking up to the top of Enchanted Rock," echoed a booming voice from beside me.

Since I was sitting in my wheelchair, I was only about four feet tall. I glanced behind me to see who was talking, and all I saw were legs—huge legs. I began looking up slowly. It seemed like seconds before my eyes finally reached his head. He was very tall and unusually muscular. I was looking into the face of a strong, young man who was slender, yet I could tell he was all muscle. His large, young, muscular arms, chest and legs protruded from his shirt and shorts. His face was filled with energy. I turned back the other way and looked up toward Enchanted Rock and acknowledged that my friends were already well on their way.

Without really thinking he was saying anything particularly

difficult, he asked a matter-of-fact question: "How would you like to go to the top?"

Of course, I thought he was kidding and just smiled and chuckled in his direction. But when I looked into his face, it was obvious he meant business. He continued, "My name is Taley Muery, and this is my friend Solar Smith. I believe between the two of us, we can get you up there."

I shook hands with Taley and Solar before asking them some questions about this ridiculous idea. I was probably just trying to humor them.

"What about all the rocks between here and the upper smooth part of Enchanted Rock?" I asked, not really giving credibility to his notion.

"Shoot, I play football at Texas University. If I couldn't carry a little weight up this hill, I wouldn't be on the team!"

A little weight? I weighed over two hundred pounds! I looked longingly up toward the mountain one more time. There was approximately a couple of hundred yards of boulders, a narrow trail and steep steps near the top. Beyond that was the smooth part of the rock face, but it was between a 20 and 30 percent grade. Even if he could somehow propel me to that point, I would not have enough traction to push on my wheels. I was about to tell him it was going to be impossible, when I looked into his eyes. He honestly wanted to do this for me as badly as I wanted to go.

"Look," I began, "why don't you help me get to the bottom of the mountain itself? Then we'll call it a day."

"Okay, but I really think we can go much farther than that!"

I did not want to dispel his enthusiasm, so I just shook my head yes. I was planning on telling him when he was absolutely exhausted that we had gone far enough. Secretly I wanted to go to the top as badly as he wanted to take me, but I didn't want to say too much so he wouldn't think I was disappointed later, if we had to turn around. We began our journey and within minutes reached a small clearing at the beginning of the trail and I looked up at the mountain. All fourteen hundred feet of it towered over us. Just then, I recognized two of the people starting their ascent up the smooth rock face. It was Mike and Rock. They were looking back at me with disbelief in their eyes. The last time they saw me, I was under the pavilion reading a book. Now here I was pushing my chair along a rocky trail. We waved at each other, and then they disappeared behind some rocks.

I examined the trail high above us and saw a long narrow rock passage where the the trail made its way through. I knew I was going to have to stop at that point. There was no way to get a wheelchair through the rocky terrain. Taley and I started again. Soon we came to an area covered with boulders. Deep crevices were between the boulders. There was no way to push my wheelchair across them, so we stopped to investigate our next move.

"You don't plan on catapulting me across this ravine, do you?" I asked with a crooked smile, hoping he knew it was a joke. He was definitely strong enough to play the ever-popular "throw the paraplegic" game.

He just smiled, and the never-say-die Taley said, "Here is where I start carrying you!" I mentioned before, I weigh over two hundred pounds. Before I could utter a word of caution, Taley was stooping down in front of me piggyback style and waving for me to get on.

"Are you kidding? I lift weights, too. I am much too heavy for you to carry me on your back," I said with a look of dismay that he even thought he could carry me.

"Get on right now," he said sternly.

"Yes, sir," I returned, hoping he knew what he was doing. I leaned forward, put my arms over his shoulders, and he stood up as if I was a small sack of potatoes. Since I have little movement from the waist down, I could not wrap my legs around his waist. I had to support all of my weight with my arms, and Taley had to lean over forward to keep from falling backward. He took several steps before coming to one of the crevices. He didn't even pause. He just lunged forward with everything he had, and stepped a full three feet. Everything seemed to go into slow motion for me. If he slipped, I was going to be seriously hurt on the jagged rocks all around us. Somehow, he made it! He repeated this process several more times before we crossed all of the crevices. I sat down and began pushing again. Taley had to carry me three more times while his friend Solar carried the chair. We finally made it to a point in the steep terrain where I knew we were going to have to stop. We looked up at the large boulders that blocked our path. A narrow path made its way past them. It was so steep and narrow it was going to be impossible to continue. I waited for this realization to sink in for Taley.

Mr. Johnson to the Rescue

Just then, an elderly man walked up and began talking to us. He was in his sixties and had a weathered appearance. His name was Mr. Johnson. He saw that we were making preparations for the ascent and wanted to give us the benefit of his wisdom and experience. We were glad he did. He went on to explain what he knew of the trails and inclines of Enchanted Rock. He was very knowledgeable about the area, having made the hike several times. His descriptions of some important details of the hill were very helpful; these details surely would have eluded us because of the limited view from our position.

After some small talk, he said, "I have a friend in a wheelchair. His name is Bobby, and I have brought him up here. As a matter of fact, I have carried him to the base of the mountain. He is very small and light. Maybe with the three of us working together, we can get you that far. I have always wanted to carry Bobby to the top, but the rock is so steep there was no way to get the leverage to push him up." He paused and was noticeably moved by the memory of his friend Bobby.

"Come on," he continued, "we are going to get you as far as possible up this mountain for Bobby."

With this incentive, we began our journey. Mr. Johnson led the way and showed us the best possible trail for a wheelchair. It was a lot of work. With my pushing on the wheels as hard as I could and with Taley pushing with his strong legs, we were making slow progress.

"This is where I brought Bobby several times," Mr. Johnson said as if talking to himself.

When Mr. Johnson turned and looked at the majestic view below, we also turned to join him. It was as if he was there physically, but mentally, he was years in the past remembering something. Mr. Johnson continued talking not even aware we were listening.

"Bobby never let on, but I knew he wanted to continue, but

couldn't. We used to sit here and enjoy the view for hours. Bobby is older now and weaker than he used to be."

I could tell by his downturned mouth and quivering lips that he was near tears. It was obvious he was wishing he had taken Bobby to the top when he was younger and stronger. He probably could have done so then.

"I have diabetes myself now and have to be careful not to overexert myself," Mr. Johnson added.

He paused before continuing. I couldn't help but feel sorry for him. He was probably thinking something like, *Why didn't I accomplish what I could while I was still able? I kept putting off until tomorrow what I should have done today.*

Mr. Johnson stopped talking because of something in his throat. His emotions had gotten the better of him. I looked over at Taley and Solar. Words did not have to be said; we all knew what we had to do. I spoke, but I spoke for the three of us.

"Mr. Johnson, we are going to climb this mountain for Bobby and for you! If it takes us all day, we won't give up! It's too important!"

Mr. Johnson told us, "Whether you make it or not, I'll tell Bobby about you," looking away again and clearing his throat. He could not do too much, but in his own way, he was getting a second chance to help Bobby climb Enchanted Rock. He was not going to let another opportunity slip by. With Bobby in mind, our strength returned and we began again.

Taley carried me over two-foot-high boulders requiring one step at a time. This meant he had to put one foot on the rock and step up with our combined weights. With one final burst of energy, Taley made his way past the last crevice before setting me back in my wheelchair. He was exhausted and sat down, too, breathing heavily. We looked up at Enchanted

Rock and knew that the real work still lay ahead.

After a brief rest, I placed my hands on the wheels, and Taley and Solar positioned themselves behind my wheelchair. Each of them had their hands on one of the handles on the backrest. Taley motioned for us to start. I began pushing on the wheels while they pushed on the back. We made slow headway. The hill was so steep that without being pushed from behind, my wheels would have just spun helplessly. Not only were they pushing, but they were keeping my chair from flipping over backwards.

We inched our way up the 25- to 30-degree slopes. We stopped every fifty feet to catch our breath. As tired as we were, we couldn't quit. We were not only climbing for our own satisfaction; we were climbing for Bobby. The seconds passed into minutes, then minutes passed into hours. We were beginning to get sunburned and sore. Over two hours had elapsed before we rolled to the bottom of the last summit. By then my arms were aching, and Taley and Solar were panting and sweating. Our water was almost gone! To make matters even worse, my two front tires had come off and I was rolling on two plastic wheel hubs. Could we go on?

Has Anyone Seen a Paraplegic?

Meanwhile, Mike, Rock, Wanice, Sandra and Julie had already gone over the top. They investigated a lake and cave on the opposite side and were back at the bottom. But because they took a different route down and back, they never passed me. They returned to the pavilion, but no Rob. They went to the van, no Rob. They went on to the Ranger Station, no Rob.

Rock was not sure how to explain to my wife that her husband had vanished, so he tried speaking to the ranger about the problem.

"I'm not sure how to say this, but a man in a wheelchair is missing!"

"Well, where did you leave him?" the ranger asked with amusement.

"Over two hours ago, we left him at the pavilion at the base of Enchanted Rock. When we returned, he was gone. We did see him begin one of the trails, but he could not have gone very far."

"You go look where you last saw him. I'll use my radio and see if any of the other rangers have seen him."

The ranger chuckled as Rock walked away. The ranger was probably wondering, *How do you lose a man in a wheelchair out here in all of these rocks and hills?*

Rock left the station, found Mike and started following the trail they had last seen me on. Sure enough, they saw wheelchair marks in the dirt. They followed them as best they could between the large flat boulders. Soon they came to a wide crevice. They looked at each other, and looked on the other side. Sure enough, the tracks were on the other side as well. They were a little confused as to how a guy in a wheelchair could have jumped across, but they just shrugged their shoulders and continued tracking.

Soon they followed the tracks to a narrow passage between the rocks that angled steeply upwards. They looked down and around and sure enough, the tracks had stopped. They looked up through the passageway and then looked at each other. "No, he couldn't have gone up that way," Mike said aloud, looking up the hill. Rock shook his head "no," and they turned around and headed down looking for other wheelchair tracks. At the bottom they met the ranger again.

"Have you seen our friend?" Rock asked the ranger.

"No, I haven't, but a bunch of other people have," he paused, then said, "Your friend is making his way to the top with the aid of a couple of guys. Believe it or not, he's almost to the top now! He's not only the first guy in a wheelchair to get lost here, he's the first paraplegic to ever climb this hill."

Mike and Rock returned to the wives waiting under the pavilion. When Mike and Rock explained to them where I was, they were *not* amused. As a matter of fact, Wanice got downright angry (understandably so).

"So, Rob is on the way to the top. He's probably reinjuring his foot and wrecking his new wheelchair," Wanice said.

"Not only that," Julie continued, "he's got my binoculars. We can't even watch him!"

"That's nothing," Sandra continued, "he's got the keys to the van. We can't even get a Coke or get in out of this heat!"

Needless to say, I was not a very popular man at that moment.

The Finish from the Heart

In the meantime, I was on the last leg of the ascent. I began getting vibes from my wife. She was physically over a mile away, but I was hearing her loud and clear.

"Guys, we have a decision to make. I'm sure my friends are down below looking for me, and I just realized I have their van keys. They can't even get a drink. Do we continue? Are we being selfish here?"

Taley spoke up, "I don't want to give up now! Rob, we have to finish this since we are so near the top! It's your call, though."

It was my decision. Taley waited for my answer. I realized that I had probably made an unwise choice in even trying to roll to the top of the hill. The question was, did I stop now or continue? I was not sure but I knew that if I stopped, I would feel like a quitter. I decided to go on! (I know now that rolling to the top was a noble idea, but not a very smart or considerate one. Not only was I physically unprepared for the challenge, I was inconveniencing my wife and some very dear friends terribly by my impulsive decision to scale the rock. I was being selfish with my goals at the expense of others.)

The last part of the trek was very steep. We rested for a few moments, then proceeded. Getting up the last part of the mountain took us twenty more minutes. But we made it! When we went over the top, a small group who had been watching our progress greeted us with applause. We rested for fifteen minutes at the top and admired the beautiful view and our surroundings. Two rangers walked up and radioed down below that we were all right. They, too, were excited that I made it.

Taley and Solar looked for a few of their friends from the University of Texas who were with them. They wanted to show them what they had done. More importantly, they wanted help in getting me back to the bottom! Both of them were exhausted. Their young strong bodies had given all they could, but we still had to get back down. However, their friends were nowhere to be found. Taley and Solar breathed deeply and we started again. It was surprisingly simple to begin the trip down the hill; I turned my wheelchair south and took off. We backed down the steep grade incredibly fast. I prayed Taley and Solar would have sure footing. If my wheelchair went out of control, I would be little more than a runaway truck with no means of stopping other than a spectacular crash.

The ascent required three hours; the descent only took a half hour. Once again, Taley carried me across the crevices and through the narrow passages. A small group greeted us at the bottom. My friends didn't know whether to hug me or hit me. After Wanice saw I was okay and that my new wheelchair was only slightly damaged, she was a little less upset.

Over to the side stood Mr. Johnson. He was absolutely speechless. He gave us the thumbs-up and wiped a tear from his eye. I realized that I could have still been sitting at the bottom of the mountain feeling sorry for myself, but if I had, Mr. Johnson would not have been so encouraged that day. I also learned so much about friendship and sacrifice from my three new friends. They went to the hill to have a good time, not help a paraplegic climb a mountain. All three of them were truly good Samaritans.

I found myself short of enough words to thank Taley, Solar and Mr. Johnson for their help. What could I say, other than "Thank you!" They worked so hard to help me that day. I will never forget them!

After apologizing to my friends for taking so long, we returned to the van for a drink of water and to celebrate. I tried explaining why I had made the hike. But unless they had seen the look in Mr. Johnson's eyes, or Taley's determination, mere words couldn't explain it. I mumbled a few words of apology and explanation, then gave up. Probably not until they read this account would they understand what had happened on Enchanted Rock that day and how much I appreciate their understanding.

The Dynamic Duo

A couple of years ago, I spoke at a youth summer camp outside of Henderson, Texas, by the name of Camp Heuwani. I spoke at night and then joined the young people during the day for some of the wackiest, funniest events I've ever been a part of.

One of the wildest events was the "blob," an air-filled tube at the edge of a pond. The objective was to jump off of a platform onto the blob while maintaining balance well enough to stay on top of the quivering, bouncing blob of air. The challenge for me was climbing to the top of the platform and hurling myself off with my arms. If successful, the next person jumped on and tried to knock the first person off while maintaining his own balance. This continues for as many times as it takes for all of the participants to be sent flying through the air and into the murky water below.

Perhaps the most popular event, though, was the ropes course. The course contained several different apparatus, including a network of ropes that began on the top of a telephone pole. The ropes and cables went through several trees and culminated in a cable slide. The kids would walk on one cable and hold onto another one with their hands. This tested balance and confidence. I watched as several of the kids did this, but noticed that many kids were too scared to try. I knew

I had to try in order to encourage them. Although I only made it about a third of the way, all of the kids tried it, and most of them made it.

Next to the ropes course was the "dynamic duo." The dynamic duo was a series of four ten-foot-long telephone poles that were suspended perpendicularly above the ground with huge cables. The first pole was seven feet off of the ground. Another seven feet separated each of the other poles. This made the top pole twenty-eight feet above the ground. The objective was for two people (i.e., the dynamic duo) to put on separate harnesses, and together climb to the top and ring a bell. The method was for the stronger of the two to climb up on the first pole and pull the second one up. Then the first would climb onto the second pole and once again pull the second person up again. This was repeated four times. A good time to do this was two minutes; however, we had a few tremendous athletes there that week. The camp record was an incredible forty-nine seconds. Two young people there that weekend were Duff Mansinger and Collen Hughes. They did the dynamic duo in fifty-seven seconds. Next, Randy and Howie did it in fifty-three seconds. Not to be outdone, Duff and Collen did it again and tied the camp record of forty-nine seconds. Randy and Howie rested for an hour then did it in an unbelievable forty-seven seconds, establishing a new camp record.

My son Jonathan was with me that week and did all of the events even though he was younger than the rest of the campers. He really wanted to do the dynamic duo but he was much too small to even reach from one pole to the next. I was surprised when Collen volunteered to help Jonathan. I was surprised for two reasons. First, it surprised me that a big boy would care to help a much younger camper for no other reason than to help. Second, I knew Collen wanted to try the dynamic duo again later with Duff and try to break their record again. Collen was willing to use his precious energy helping Jonathan, even knowing it might hurt his own time later. I rolled over to him and whispered to him, "When we put the welfare of others ahead of our own desires, God will bless our efforts."

It amazed me that Collen was sincerely interested in helping Jonathan. Collen struggled to pull Jonathan from pole to pole and they finished in about five minutes. Collen was young and very strong, but he didn't have any strength left when he and Jonathan came down. Collen rested for ten minutes, then he and Duff put the harnesses on again. When the counselor blew the whistle, Collen stood up on Duff's leg and pulled himself up on the first pole and extended his arm to Duff in one flowing movement. He yanked Duff up, who then stood up, and Collen jumped up to the next pole with Duff pushing him up. Once again, Collen pulled himself up on the second pole and extended his arm to Duff in one flowing movement. They repeated this maneuver two more excruciating times. When Collen reached the top he rang the bell with a grunt. The counselor stopped the watch and with wide eyes screamed, "A new camp record-forty-five seconds!"

Collen discovered firsthand how God blesses our efforts when we put the welfare of others ahead of our own and work together for a common good.

PART III

Running Your Own Race

Chapter 6

Setting Your Goal

Do not be anxious for tomorrow; for tomorrow will care for itself. Each day has enough trouble of its own.

—Matthew 6:34

Two Solid "Goal" Truths

Hopefully, you have gathered from the preceding chapters that overcoming adversity requires the right frame of mind. Now that you are hopefully looking at life with a positive perspective, it's time to actively pursue your goals. Although the idea of learning to set goals and achieve them is universal, individuals have very different ideas about what constitutes a challenge for them. I set a goal to walk despite paralysis. Someone else who is facing a chronic illness may go for the goal of maintaining a positive outlook instead of a negative frame of mind. Someone whose business is failing may set a goal of showing a profit six months down the line. Someone in an unhappy marriage could decide their goal is to seek counseling just for themselves, if their spouse won't go, or maybe decide to learn better skills to open the lines of communication between them.

- First of all, choose one or just a few goals at a time. There is no way to do anything well when we have too many goals at one time—it's overwhelming. (That's why experts don't recommend trying to quit smoking and trying to lose weight at the same time.)

- Second, finish one task before moving on to the next.

When we don't use this time-management tool, we will find ourselves frustrated, doing so many different tasks that it's too difficult to finish anything. These simple time- and resource-management skills are necessary to accomplish our goals despite adversity. After narrowing the list down to the few tasks, we can begin to think about accomplishing our goals. (I struggle with this as I try tackling too much at once. My family helps me with this one!)

However, don't just jump into it without thought. A common mistake is to begin before thinking about what we need. Charging ahead without a proper plan gets you nowhere, except discouraged, maybe. Properly prepare yourself for the goal. If it requires training, then train. If it requires studying, then study. Have a single-minded purpose when pursuing your goals. Setting the goal to walk again after a fifty-five-foot fall and suffering a severed spinal cord was very tough. Soon after, I received second-degree burns from the knees down. Then I had to have another back surgery, and I had many other difficulties associated with this major operation. If I had allowed circumstances to sway my thinking, I would have never been able to attain my goal of walking. This may all seem a little overwhelming, but most of us only need to work on a few of the areas this book covers. The others probably come naturally to you. My strengths and weakness are different from yours, so the areas we need to work on are different also.

Once you have set the goal, and prepared yourself for it, decide right now that you are not going to quit. If you approach your goal with the attitude that "I'll try and see what happens," you've already lost. Goals that begin this way are destined to fail. Marriages that begin this way will surely end in divorce. Give it everything you have, and don't ever quit until you have exhausted every possibility. If you give it everything you have and are unsuccessful, that's okay. You've done your best!

In one of the chapters that follow, we will talk more about counting the cost, but I must introduce this concept while talking about goal setting. Recently, I had conflicting goals I wanted to pursue. I was obsessed with them! They were all I could think about. When I went to sleep they were the last thought on my mind. When I awoke, they were my first thought. I dreamed about them, I planned for them, I wanted them. Because of their magnitude, the two goals could not be accomplished simultaneously or concurrently. The first goal was to earn a master's degree. This may seem like a simple goal to some people, but I graduated in the middle of my high school class and was a very average student. Despite this fact, I have already earned two undergraduate degrees. Earning a master's degree was a goal that my family supported and would help me achieve. The second goal was to earn another world record. This would entail using a hand-cycle (hand-powered bicycle) to travel 10,500 miles in a counter-clockwise trip around the perimeter of the entire United States. For the sake of simplicity, I will analyze the latter goal in terms of the following goal-setting questions.

Five Goal-Setting Questions

1. Is it a viable goal?
2. Can I visualize the steps?
3. What are the costs?

4. Can I pay the price?

5. Do I believe in it enough not to quit when it gets tough?

Answer to question one: Yes, it was a viable goal. My goal was another trip similar to the Row Across America, which you will read about in chapter 9. I learned so much on the first trip, I was sure I could apply what I had learned and make this next trip even better. It was also something that I could use to benefit me, charities, my family and the millions of people I hoped to encourage and inspire along the way.

Answer to question two: Yes, I could visualize the steps and how I would accomplish the goal. I had the maps outlined and knew the cities I would pass through. I had letters prepared for a huge mailing along with a database of the zip codes. Last, I bought a hand-cycle with which to make the trip. I trained very hard to increase my mileage to 100 miles per day with the hand-cycle. I participated in several long races (one was 150 miles), and the TV networks even covered the finishes of some of them. Mentally, physically and spiritually I could visualize the steps.

Answer to question three: The costs were staggering. I would have to leave my job and depend strictly upon renumerations from the speaking engagements. After the trip was over, I might have to find another job if I lost mine in the process. I was weighing all of this and was not sure if I was willing to pay such a high price. I asked my family what they thought. If they were for it, I would probably do it. The response shocked me!

"You will have to leave us again for a nine-month period. I guess you have to ask the question: Who do you love more—us or the self-gratification of another accomplishment?"

I was shocked at my wife's response. I thought she was

overdramatizing the situation, but the more I thought about it, I realized she was right. For the rest of our short days together, my family would either know I chose "them" or I chose "me." I also had to remember my wife and I do not think alike. I often think about conquests and victories in terms of physical abilities and outward displays of overcoming obstacles. My wife, on the other hand, often thinks of victories in terms of her relationship with her family and friends. A victory for her was a loving family and a warm home. I was choosing my kind of victory over hers. What kind of an example would this be for my family? It is one thing to accomplish our goals with the support of our families. But it is selfish to put our own goals over the corporate good of our family, nation and God. Our country was based upon the principle we have individual freedoms, but they should not be contrary to the corporate good.

Answer to question four: No, I could not pay the price. It was too high! I could not accomplish this goal without hurting my family. If the choice was between my goal and my family's well-being, I had no decision to make. My family had to come first.

Answer to question five: I didn't have to ask question number five. This is not to say I would never accomplish the goal. The cost could change at a later date, and I'll ask the questions again. When the answer to one of the questions is no, it could mean "no for now," not "no forever."

Which goal did I try to attain? I refused to set a goal that would cost me more than I wanted to pay. I would not sacrifice my family for any goal! Greater problems can result from putting your own selfish desires ahead of your loved one's needs. Therefore, my family and I decided I would pursue the master's degree as time and money allowed. As a matter of fact, I finished it a few years ago, and it opened many doors for me at my job. I am now a vice president in my company. My earning a graduate degree also helped my family in terms of income. I put my family first, and God blessed the decision and the results were awesome.

The next three chapters are very important in learning to overcome adversity. Failing to do the things covered in these chapters is a common mistake and can lead to failure. These chapters discuss visualizing the steps, counting the cost and paying the price. With these very important truths, you are on your way to achieving your goals. Remember that overcoming adversity is an ongoing process. Recovering alcoholics overcome adversity on a daily basis. It is not a once-and-for-all victory. It requires small victories each day. But the very first step is determining and setting your goal. After all, if you don't know where you're going, how will you know when you get there?

Here are a few steps to help you with goal setting:

- List your goals on separate lists. One each for the day, the week, the month, the year and lifetime goals.

- Scratch off the ones that are not viable at this time (this may change later).

- Prioritize your goals.

- Once you've established your goals, list the steps you need to take to achieve them.

- List the costs of each goal.

- Ensure you can pay the price of each goal.

- Keep records and/or before-and-after photos or lists, so that you can see what you are accomplishing. With each accomplishment ticked off, you will grow in confidence.

- Ensure your list of goals is balanced. You should have goals in all areas of your life—for instance, your personal, spiritual, financial and professional life.

- Go!

Chapter 7

Visualizing the Steps

You have to learn the rules of the game. And then you have to play better than anyone else.

—Senator Dianne Feinstein

Know the Rules of the Game

This principle may sound simplistic, but if you want to enjoy success in any area of your life, you need to know how to play the game. I cannot get up and run away from my wheelchair—gravity works and my leg muscles don't. Gravity rules. However, I did learn to walk with the aid of leg braces and crutches. To get to that point, however, I had to learn some new rules about developing upper-body strength, stamina and the endurance to enable me to "stand" despite my paralysis. God gives us rules for life, too: the Ten Commandments. His gamebook is the Bible. No matter what your difficulty in life, there's a certain maturity that comes along with the knowledge and acceptance that, if you want to play, you've got to play by—and know—the rules.

When I decided I wanted to set a World Record for walking by a paraplegic and a Guinness World Record for long-distance rowing, I had to follow strict requirements. If I had skipped a step, or neglected to document my progress correctly, even if I had physically accomplished what I set out to do I would not have been successful. This became very frustrating at times, as you'll read later in Part III, but "going by the book" was necessary as in any area of life, whether you're in a boardroom or on a baseball diamond.

A "Touchdown" in Baseball

When the boys were younger, I coached their T-ball teams. For those of you who have never seen a T-ball game, you have missed out on one of the most hilarious and entertaining hours of your life. The kids who play are from ages four to six. They are barely able to catch, throw or run, much less understand who's winning or how to make an out.

Often the only ones who take the game seriously are the parents who act like their sons or daughters are future Hall-of-Famers because they can run the bases while picking their noses. I coached for four years and thought I had seen it all. I saw little boys stand and watch the ball roll past while looking at the clouds or waving to a parent who is screaming at them to get the ball. I've seen a little girl picking flowers in the outfield as the ball rolled right up to her feet. I've seen kids run from home plate to second base. I've seen excited kids run from third base right over to Mommy and Daddy, never getting close to home plate. The funniest play I have ever seen, however, happened when one of the mothers insisted that her son knew how to play, despite the fact that he had never been to a single practice. I wanted him to sit out the first game so that he could watch the other boys and girls and learn from them. She was so persistent that I begrudgingly agreed to let him play. I should have heeded my own rules and not made an exception. This was a capital mistake!

When it was his turn to bat, he stepped up to the plate and the ball was placed on top of the tee. He took careful aim and indeed hit the ball past second base. I was pleasantly surprised. After hitting the ball, however, he just stood there.

"Run!" I screamed.

He finally started running and ran to first base and just stood there despite the fact that the other team had not even begun to field the ball. Despite my screams and the corporate screams of the parents, he proceeded to just stand there. After the ball was returned to the pitcher, I called time-out.

"Dusty, why did you just stand there on first base?"

"I don't know," he said, grinning from ear to ear because he made it to first base.

"Listen, when the next batter gets a hit, you run to second base. If I say 'Go,' then run to third. If I say 'Keep going,' run to home plate. Do you know where second base is?"

"Yep," he said, pointing in the right direction.

"Do you know where third base is?"

"Yep," he said, pointing.

"Do you know where home plate is?"

"Yep," he said, pointing.

"Okay, then. When I say go, you go."

"Okay!"

The next child came to the plate and hit the ball very close to first base. I yelled, "Go!"

Instead of heading for second base, Dusty ran over to the ball, picked it up, tagged out his own teammate, then ran with the ball around all of the bases, finally stepping on home plate where he yelled triumphantly, "Touchdown!"

Suddenly there was an eruption of laughter from the umpire, both teams, all of the coaches (including me) and all of the parents and spectators on both sides. There were only two people not laughing—Dusty and his mother. I never let another child play during a game until I saw them at practice, because not everything in life can be accepted at face value.

❋ ❋ ❋

After you know the rules, you need to visualize the steps necessary to accomplish that goal. By visualizing the steps we need to be able to see how we get from one step to the other. These steps must be connected *and* associated. They must be connected so you can go from one to another. They must be associated so that there is continuity in the steps. Often, our goals become so tough we have to take just one step at a time. If you find that your goal is really big, just focus on the next step ahead of you, not the whole daunting journey. Professional football teams do this. If they are three games from going to the Super Bowl, they only concentrate on the next game, not the Super Bowl itself. Have you heard that riddle about "How do you eat an elephant?" The answer is "One bite at a time." Anything, no matter how scary, can be manageable if you take it one piece or one step at a time.

We must be able to get from where we are to where we want to be, but first we have to know where we are going. Give this a lot of thought; don't just jump into it. My first physical step as a paraplegic was an extremely emotional one. As you have already read, I set the goal to walk again after a catastrophic injury. But in order to accomplish this, I had to complete an eighteen-point list, one grueling step at a time. The goal was so large that I had to dissect it into smaller parts. Many of us never accomplish our goals because we set them, then we just go in circles without any real plan of attack. Others set a goal and then wait for our ship to come in. I've got a better idea—swim out to it! Take the initiative to follow your dream; don't wait for it to come true by accident or luck. Set a series of connected goals and then begin accomplishing them one at a time. Don't try to accomplish them all at once; you'll just set yourself up for failure. Pace yourself.

When I was in the U.S. Air Force, there was a young man who was thirty pounds overweight. Everyone in our squadron had to run a mile and a half in twelve minutes. This is not a very difficult time to make, but for this man it was a monumental task. He saw I was the fastest man in our squadron, so he asked me to help him. He knew if he was not able to do this in just two weeks, he would be discharged from the service and have to go home a defeated man. I agreed to help him. After watching him run, I discovered he was making a common error in distance running. He was not pacing himself. He would dash until exhausted, rest briefly and then dash again. I instructed him to slow down and pace himself. He would actually finish faster if he slowed down and didn't burn all of his energy in short bursts. Within days, he was doing better and finished boot camp with the rest of us.

While we can accomplish our goals one step at a time, we also must be able to visualize the next several steps. Otherwise, the steps will be disjointed. Imagine that your goal is to cross a stream by jumping from one rock to another. Before you begin, you must ensure that the route you have chosen has rocks close enough all the way across the stream for you to complete the journey. Otherwise, you will find yourself in the middle of the creek without a clear path to the other side. You will have to retreat and try again. Be sure that you can visualize every single step of the goal before tackling the first step.

Put One Foot in Front of the Other— Repeat as Often as Necessary

Once you visualize your goal and the necessary steps to get you there, you need to get started. The Miracle Walk only happened because I was willing to take the next step. Each of us has a choice to stay where we are, or take just one more step in the direction we want to go. It is sometimes overwhelming to think of where you want to be relative to where you are now. Don't think to yourself, *I have so far to go, why even try?* If you eventually want to go over a mountain, don't even think about how big it is or even how far you have to go just to get to it. The first move is to start out in the general direction. Don't think of the number of steps—just take one in the right direction. Normally, that step is so easy that it builds our confidence to take another, then another. Soon we might find ourselves running over the mountain. Most mountains are not nearly as scary as they look anyway. Once we begin the climb we often wonder what we were afraid of. Even when the climb is hard, if we just take one step at a time, it is doable.

After my second back surgery, I was in the Stryker frame that rotated me continuously to keep the pressure off of my back and spine. It also made me feel seasick, terrified of falling all over again, disoriented and bored to tears. I could not even imagine the pain and discomfort of an entire day (much less a week) in this torture chamber, so I thought to myself, *I can do this for the next hour.* Then after that hour, I thought again, *I can do this for another hour.* Soon the hours, days and week passed.

Everyone faces crises. The happiest people I know are those

who can take them in stride. It is the mighty oak that breaks because it is not capable of bending. Sometimes you need to bend, sometimes you need to move, and sometimes you just need to accept what life throws at you. Once you resolve where you are, and where you want to go, just take the next step.

Recently I literally flew around the world on a business trip. I flew over thirty-five thousand miles. I did this safely and comfortably in huge airplanes made of steel weighing tons. This was made possible because of the first step in 1903 in Kitty Hawk, North Carolina, when two brothers flew less than one hundred feet! It is staggering what can be accomplished in the long run, but it all starts with one small step. You can do it—take that next step. You will soon rise above the adversity that is keeping you down just as gravity was keeping the Wright brothers down. Just as gravity is an adversity to an airplane, your adversity is something you can overcome, even though it is still present. Some adversity is always present; we just have to take the first step despite it. My paralysis is still here. In the same way, you cannot change who your parents are, the disease you may have, the death of loved ones, etc. You must operate within the parameters given to you in life.

Don't be overwhelmed at the task before you; just take one step at a time, one day at a time, one goal at a time. You can do it!

Here are a few helpful keys to get you started:

- Start by taking one small step in the right direction.

- Begin taking larger steps as your confidence grows. Eventually you will be running.

- Normally the step you need to take is obvious. Often there is only one direction to go. Your first instinct is usually the right answer. However, if you don't know what to do, make a list of all of the possible steps you might take from right where you are at this moment of crisis or indecision. Really brainstorm about this. There are no dumb suggestions at this point. Be creative with the list. Then scratch through the ideas you don't think are pratical or you don't feel ready to take just yet. Once you have the list down to a few suggestions, choose one and do it. Don't be discouraged. Even if it does not go well, then at least you've eliminated one option and are narrowing down the possibilities. Then take one more step on the list instead, then another. See where this takes you. I've got news for you: Moving in some direction is almost always better than not moving at all. If you find yourself moving in the wrong direction, go back to your list and try another alternative.

- Be sure to list every one of the steps from where you are to the realization of the goal. In other words, think and plan before you act.

- Ensure each step connects to the next. Ensure the steps are associated so that there is continuity in the steps (i.e., you are accomplishing what you really want to accomplish).

- Ensure your steps do not infringe on the rights of others.

- If you feel as if you're ready to give up, ask for spiritual strength to help you persevere.

Chapter 8

Counting the Cost

There is no such thing as a free lunch.

—*Author Unknown*

Y ou get what you pay for!" We have all heard this before, and it is so true. Consequently, the loftier your goal, the greater the cost. Tell an Olympian the cost is low to achieve a gold medal in the Olympics and the Olympian will beg to differ. He or she probably rose at 5:00 or 6:00 A.M. and trained for twelve straight hours. The Olympian probably doesn't even live at home, but rather in a camp with other Olympic hopefuls. The cost of success can require years of intense, dedicated training. Is it a price you are willing to pay? It is better to count the cost and then either resize the goal to fit in the boundary of your budget, or expand your budget. When I say "budget," I mean this generically. It can represent time, money, sweat, training or education, etc.

What if the cost is too high? We each have to answer that question individually. For example, the cost may be so high that I risk my health or family. Am I willing to pay that kind of price? My answer is no, but you'll have to answer the question for yourself. Many people have answered yes to this question. They have accomplished their goals, but at what cost?

Someone recently commented to me that a few of my accomplishments are impressive. But then this person asked me the following questions: Where is your family in all of this? Do you have any time for them? Do you set any goals that relate to your family? What price do they pay for your goals? Is your goal setting and determination to overcome purely individualistic, no matter what the cost to others?

Several years ago, Jonathan put my priorities into their proper place. It started when I returned from a rather lengthy tour of work and speaking engagements. I hadn't seen my family for ten straight days. My wife understood I had to fulfill my obligations associated with my job at DynCorp. However, in addition to my regular job, several speaking engagements were stacked on top of each other. It was the only time these particular appointments could be made. I was tired, and my wife was tired of me being away, but somehow we prevailed. The evening I returned, I was tucking my boys in bed. We had already said our prayers and I told them a few of their favorite stories. It was then, on January 6, that my youngest son, Jonathan, asked me *the* question.

Dad, What Are Your Goals?

"Dad, here it is the beginning of another year. What are your goals for this upcoming year?" I contemplated his question thoughtfully. I was proud of him for thinking in terms of goal setting. Both Jason and Jonathan are goal setters. Jason has won about every award given in track at his school, is an excellent student and is a U.S. Marine. Jonathan is extremely gifted as a student and has set his sights on the Naval Academy. I am convinced (even more importantly, they are convinced) that they will succeed at their goals. After several seconds of thought, I answered his question with a list of goals.

"Son, I would like to complete a few contractual items at

work. I would also like to schedule a few specific speaking engagements that eluded me last year. As you know, I am trying to finish. . . ." I continued listing a few more goals. I could tell by his response that he was not at all pleased with my answer. So I stopped and asked him the same question. In so doing, I hoped to ascertain why he was not happy with my answer.

"Son, what are your goals for this next year?"

"I'm still thinking about mine, but you know, I noticed something about your goals. I thought I would be high on your list. You didn't even mention me."

I looked at him. He was not trying to point out a flaw in my character. He was genuinely hurt that he didn't appear to fit into my top priorities at all. Of course he did, but my list of goals did not seem to indicate this. His question began a lengthy thought process for me that lasted all night. As I lay in bed, I asked myself if I had let my priorities get out of balance. I decided Jonathan was right. I had neglected my family. The price I was paying to accomplish a few of my goals was too high. I realized how soon my sons would be off on their own and wondered what they would remember about my priorities.

The following morning, I apologized to my family for the lack of attention I had paid them. But I knew it meant nothing unless I was prepared to change, to back it up with some action. Within the course of the next several weeks, I adjusted my schedule. I didn't give up on my goals, I just put off a few of them until a later time. I decided that I had too many goals, and my family was suffering because of it. My family and I also went on several long weekend getaways. I also spent much of my free time with my boys individually by going to a movie, or taking some father-and-son getaways like skiing or camping. Jonathan didn't have to say anything else to me about it. His countenance changed as he saw that I was not only spending quality time with him, but I was prepared to balance his needs against my goals.

To "Bee" or Not to "Bee"

Once you have decided upon your goals, you need to contemplate if you're willing to pay the price to go after them.

"Dad, it fell! The old tree has fallen," I yelled as I ran up the long driveway to our old country house. It was autumn in upper New York, and a cool breeze blew toward the house. The grass was starting to die. The trees were beginning to turn every shade of red, orange and brown imaginable. All of these signs of the coming winter completely eluded me as I continued to run up the driveway.

I was filled with excitement, but greater still was a fear that ran cold in my veins. I had escaped one of my greatest fears by a few feet and mere seconds.

"Dad, the old tree has fallen," I yelled one last time as I rounded the corner and headed into the porch. I ran into Dad who was coming outside to see what the commotion was.

"Slow down, Rob. What is it? What tree has fallen?"

"The bee tree! The big hollow bee tree. The storm blew it over last night. I walked right by it before I saw it. There are bees everywhere."

"All right, it's okay," he said to calm me down before continuing. "Now we can have fresh honey. When I was a boy, I used to collect honey. Now you can, too. I'll fix you up so the bees cannot get to you. You'll see. This will be a real adventure for you. You'll just scoop up pounds of honey with a ladle. I can still remember the first time I collected honey from a bee tree. I was just. . . ."

As Dad started recounting his adventure once again, my mind wandered to my very first confrontation with a bee. As a matter of fact, it is my earliest memory of anything. A smile came to my face as the memory returned. Dad probably thought I was listening to his story, but my mind was traveling back ten years in time.

I was four years old and sitting on the back porch, which Dad was busy screening in. He was hammering away and didn't notice me sitting behind him watching his every move. Dad towered over me. I watched his ease at lifting heavy boards and longed to perform such feats of strength. It was late in the morning, but because it was springtime, the dew was still on the ground. New flowers were making their way to the surface, and a few of them were already blooming. This, of course, meant bees were beginning to fly from flower to flower. Mom walked onto the porch from the house carrying a tray of peanut butter sandwiches and lemonade. Dad stopped what he was doing, turned around to grab a sandwich and take a well-deserved break. As he turned, he saw me and sat down beside me to eat his sandwich. He turned on the radio and listened to an Oriole game while he ate.

I pretended to know who Frank Robinson and Boog Powell were as Dad cheered them on. We exchanged a few words (mostly he answered the irritating questions a four-year-old can ask) and we continued chomping on our sandwiches. He was in the middle of one of his answers when suddenly a large bee landed on the other side of my sandwich. I stared at the bee as it ate my sandwich. Dad was watching the bee, too, with a casual interest. He knew if I sat still, the bee would just fly away, but he had no idea what was actually in my four-year-old brain. I was not interested in just watching the bee. I was angry that this bee would be so bold as to eat my sandwich right in front of me. How dare he? I signaled to Dad that I was going to fix the bee. He had no idea what I was trying to tell him in gestures, or he certainly would have stopped me.

I slowly turned the sandwich around so the bee was on my side. I moved the sandwich slowly toward my face. The bee had no idea what was coming and neither, as it turned out, did I. Dad watched me curiously and was not overly concerned since I was moving so slowly. The bee was actually a yellow jacket, capable of biting and stinging over and over without losing its stinger. When the sandwich was just inches from my face, I quickly opened my mouth, and took a large bite. I pulled the sandwich back away from my face, and sure enough, the bee was gone. I had totally surprised the bee. I crunched down on the bread, peanut butter and insect in my mouth. It was I who was about to be surprised as I looked over at Dad. He did not have the look of approval on his face I was expecting to see. It was one of disbelief and horror. The surprise was not over yet!

In the back in my mouth, near my throat, I felt something crawling. It moved a little and then I felt as if a doctor was pulling my tonsils out without anesthetic. Then I felt a crawling sensation to the left side of my mouth. Another sharp pain filled the left side of my mouth. More crawling was followed by more pain. This process was repeated half a dozen times. I opened my mouth to spit it out. But the bee was not finished with me yet. It proceeded to crawl all over the inside of my mouth. He stung my tongue, cheeks, gums and roof of my mouth. I began to scream in terror. By this time, Dad was beside me trying to chase the bee out. After the bee was good and ready and had gotten in the last word as to whose sandwich it really was, he flew out. I continued to scream as Mom appeared on the porch. Dad told her what happened. Later, after my parents were sure I was going to survive the ordeal, they both chuckled about the incident.

My mind was startled back to the present by Dad's description of the thunder in his story as he yelled, "Clap! The thunder roared and sparks flew. Then boom, there was the tree laying down on the ground," my father continued his story.

"Dad, I've heard this story before. Come on, let's go get the honey."

"Okay, you wait here while I get the equipment we need."

There was going to be a high cost involved in collecting the honey. Was I willing to pay the price? I wasn't sure yet. But I was not going to attempt it until I counted the cost— underestimating a bee's sting had cost me dearly when I was younger. Dad disappeared into the house and came back within minutes. He had two pairs of his pants, three shirts, gloves, hat, military boots, mosquito netting, a scarf, a belt, masking tape, a bucket and large spoon.

"Here you go, Son. I'll have you fixed up in no time. Those bees will not be able to hurt you."

He proceeded to put layer after layer of the large clothes on me. Lastly, he put the hat on me, draped the mosquito netting over it and tucked the netting down into my collar. The next step was to put the scarf around my neck. He tied a belt tightly around my waist so there were no cracks for bees to crawl through. Next he used masking tape to close any potential openings in my clothing. The last touch was the thick leather gloves. He handed me the bucket and spoon and said, "Go get the honey, boy. You're ready for those bees now."

Dad knew what I was about to do was important—not only as a learning experience, but to help me overcome my fear of bees. The fear did not only stem from the sandwich episode, but from something much later. I turned and began to walk down the driveway. I was going to have to walk down the driveway, across the road and into the field on the other side. The bee tree was over one hundred yards away from me. I walked slowly. Each step rang in my covered-up ears. A fear in the pit of my stomach began to swell until I thought I would become ill. I walked along as if on a death march. The real memory of fear, which was plaguing me, began to surface. I turned and waved one more time, and Dad gave me a thumbs-up sign. I turned once again in the direction that was behind my fear.

As I began walking, I was no longer in upper New York as a fourteen-year-old. I was eleven and living in Virginia. It was spring as I was walking through a row of trees, which separated our property from our neighbor to the north. I was looking around at the green grass, the budding trees and the flowers. Looking east into the field below, I saw ducks swimming in a pond. Just days before, I saw geese as they rested before continuing their long trip north for the summer. I looked back in front of me and watched a few bees whiz by me at an incredible speed. Suddenly, they disappeared. Where had they gone? I stopped walking and explored the mystery. As I waited just a few seconds, a few more bees flew by and they too disappeared about thirty feet in front of me.

Walking forward about twenty feet, I looked around. I could not see anything, but I could hear a deep buzzing sound somewhere in front of me. I continued to scan the area in front of me and suddenly two more bees shot by me. I watched closely as they disappeared into a small hole in the ground just ten feet in front of me. I watched in amazement as bees continued flying in and out of the hole. Taking a few more steps forward to get a closer look, I could hear a dull roar of buzzing in the earth below me. I couldn't tell if it was the vibration in the ground or the sound that I was sensing the most. I discovered later that these bees were actually a strain of hornets that live in the ground.

I was not wearing a shirt, just a baggy pair of shorts. Normally, I was barefoot, but this time I was wearing tennis shoes (thank God!). Confident the shoes would protect me from a bee sting; I took one more step with my right foot toward the hole. Suddenly the ground gave way! My right foot disappeared into a cavern underground. My foot was caught! I realized all too late the reason I could feel the vibration on the ground was because the bees' nest was so large, I was actually standing on top of it. Little did I know several types of bees build their nests beneath the ground. Sometimes their nests can extend several feet in every direction from the entrance. I sank deeper into the cavern and suddenly the air around me was filled with a black cloud of buzzing. As if by an unheard charge sounded on a trumpet, they descended on me and began to sting and bite. They were stinging all over my body simultaneously. They were not only mad because I had fallen into their home, but they probably heard that I had tried to eat one of their relatives years before.

Going into shock, I yanked on my right foot several times before it was free. I turned and screamed at the top of my lungs. This was a huge mistake: The bees made a beeline for and then filled my mouth. I spit out as many as I could and began running for the house. Once I was moving at full speed, I was not being stung as much. However, the bees that were already on me clung on and continued to sting. Praise God that hornets do not sting over and over (they only sting once and then die). Their bite, however, is as painful as their sting. The last thing I remember was running toward the house at full speed and wondering how I was going to clear the fence ahead without stopping. My brain shut down because it did not want to monitor any more pain. My brother Mike told me the rest of the story later, because my brain blocked everything out but the pain. Mike was in the garden just a few feet from the fence. I knew Mike would not help me, so I didn't even bother to ask.

Without even slowing down, I jumped up and cleared a four-foot-high wood fence. My right shoe touched the top and pushed off the fence like a springboard, propelling my body through the air another ten feet before hitting the ground. I continued running at full speed toward the back of the house where my mother was standing, wondering what all of the shouting was about. Big brothers often will not help, but I instinctively knew that moms sign a contract with God. The terms of the contract were that no matter what stupid thing I did, Mom had to help me. Sure enough, seeing my predicament, she grabbed a broom and pushed me into the closed-in porch. Closing the door behind us, she proceeded to beat the bees off of my rapidly swelling body. I had been stung a hundred or so times, and the poison that filled my system caused me to begin to shake. I quickly fell to my knees as Mom beat the last of the bees off of me. Mom helped me into the living room, and I fell onto the couch. I fell asleep and shivered as my body fought off all the poison. It was three days before the swelling went down and the fever was totally gone. The fever passed, but my fear of bees increased over the years.

The Old Bee Tree: The Conclusion

"Honk!" A neighbor honked as his car went by the driveway. Suddenly, my mind was back to the present. I looked at the car, which held a few laughing neighbors. They obviously were getting a big kick out of the get-up I was wearing. They disappeared over the hill, and I turned my attention back to the tree. Crossing the road, I paused one more time before walking toward the fallen bee tree.

"You can do it!" came Dad's voice from behind me. Waving over my shoulder, I took one last deep breath before I moved closer to the tree. The decision was made—I had estimated the cost and I was willing to pay the price! Within seconds, I was a few feet away. I knew if I stopped, fear would not allow me to continue. A few steps more and I was at the fallen tree. I looked down at it. The great tree was so hollow it had broken in two as it hit the ground. The impact cracked the tree down the middle of the honeybee nest. It was cracked wide open like a back door just inviting me inside. Part of the honeycomb was in the hollow tree on the ground. The rest was still in the trunk of the tree standing to my left. The old dead oak tree had died long ago and was a perfect host for the hive.

Bees began to swarm and a few scouts landed on me to try to scare me away before the swarm had to get serious with me. Watching the scouts as they crawled around sticking their stingers through my clothes, I realized with great relief that the layers were indeed too thick for them to reach my skin. Within seconds, I was covered with angry, buzzing bees, but not one of them could get to me. I was completely impervious to their attack.

I turned and waved at Dad. All he could see was the shape of a boy deep inside a black cloud of swarming bees. Setting the bucket down, I sank the spoon deep into the honey. Now the bees descended upon me en masse, as I continued working. I fought off the fear that the bees would find some way inside my clothes. My heart began beating faster as they increased their fervor to find a way to penetrate my defenses. When the bucket was full, I picked it up and walked back toward the house. By the time I crossed the road, only a few bees remained on me. When I arrived back at the house, all of the bees were gone. Dad slapped me on the back with pride that I had not let my fears beat me. Dad emptied the bucket into a large pan, and I returned to the tree two more times to get all of the honey.

Overcoming such a small fear was not a great feat. I'm sure you have overcome greater obstacles than this. The point is, there was a cost attached to gathering the honey. Before I considered paying the price, I counted the cost. If I had succumbed to those fears, because they were greater than the price I was willing to pay, that would have been all right. An appropriate response would have been achieving the goal in a way I was willing to pay the price. In other words, adjust the size of the goal to fit the price I am willing to pay. Quitting, however, is not okay. Don't let your disregard for counting the cost ahead of time paralyze you from seeking the adventures and challenges of life. If we give up on the small challenges, it will be much easier to give up on other and bigger challenges. I have found the more we succeed, the easier it is to succeed the next time. The more we give up, however, the easier it is to give up the next time. Don't forget to count the cost before even attempting to pay the price. Forgetting to count the cost of a goal is a paralyzing mistake! Once you have counted the cost and decided that the price is not too high, then it's time to pay the price by following through toward your goal. The following chapter deals with the concept of this important concept: paying the price.

Here are a few steps to help you count the cost of your goals:

- Estimate the cost of your goals, financially and in terms of the time they will take. Be sure to include the cost of any training or education required. You should be able to pay for them without sacrificing your other responsibilities or relationships. This is especially true with shared resources in a family.

- Estimate the spiritual cost of your goals. You should ensure that these are goals that are worthy of your beliefs. If you have to rationalize very hard, they are usually not noble goals.

• Determine if they are goals that you can physically accomplish. It's okay to challenge and push yourself here. When I set the Guinness World Record for rowing, I definitely pushed myself. Your goals should not be physically dangerous, though.

• Mentally prepare yourself for the goal. Go to the library or check the Internet and learn as much as you possibly can about it.

• You have limited resources like time, money, relationships and material possessions. Use them wisely. Don't use up all of your resources trying to attain your goal. This is without a doubt important when it comes to your relationships. Be careful not to tax your family or friendships in your attempts to reach your goals. What good is achieving goals if you are alone? Who will you share your victories with?

Chapter 9

The Row Across America:
Paying the Price

I believe that if you put in the work, the results will come. I don't do things halfheartedly. Because if I do, I can expect halfhearted results.

—Michael Jordan

The "Mission Impossible"

This chapter is dedicated to my mother, Dorothy, who, by her own example, taught me the importance of sacrifice.

This is where "the rubber meets the road." In order to go for your goal, you have to pay the price! Don't let anything stop you. You will have moments of discouragement. If you attempt your goals using the methods I described, you will more than likely be successful. On the other hand, if God gives you a goal, the only thing that can stop you is you. God has given you talents, and in order to please Him and yourself, you need to use them.

Being able to walk again was a miracle. While God granted that miracle, I don't believe it would have happened if I had not done my part. With this goal under my belt, I began setting new and bigger goals. Soon after, I had a new dream: to set the Guinness World Record for long-distance rowing.

So, *I set the goal.*

Next, *I visualized the steps.* Other than my relationship with God and my family, it became the focus of all of my energy and being. I trained for years in order to attempt breaking the world's record for rowing. As a matter of fact, I was attempting to break the old Guinness World Record for rowing four times over! I was using a RowCycle (a row machine on wheels) for hours every day. I also used a stationary row machine and lifted weights relentlessly. No matter how hard I worked out, and how tired I became, I pushed myself harder. I knew the mountains and obstacles were going to be tougher than anything I had ever attempted. I gave it everything I had. I had a singleness of purpose.

I counted the cost! I made sure this was a goal my family was willing to support. It took several months before Wanice was convinced that this was a worthy goal, but eventually she was behind me 100 percent. It's not hard to understand why she was so skeptical initially. After all, she had almost lost me in the accident that changed our whole lives, and she knew how dangerous any further injury or illness, like an unnoticed kidney infection or neglected sore, could be. She also knew that she was the one who had to carry the full load of the children and home while I put in thousands of hours of training, and then traveled for months away from home.

Then I had to factor in the tremendous physical challenges. In order to row across America, I would have to pull 15,000 to 18,000 strokes on the oars per day. The average resistance was about 50 pounds per stroke, but increased to over 100 according to the slope of the road. I would also be burning 6,000 to 8,000 calories per day for 119 days. This is equivalent to walking up the stairs of the Empire State Building seven times per day, for 119 days. In addition to the rowing, I was going to speak almost every night (sometimes several times per day) of the trip to help pay for it. Given all these factors, it's not surprising that I was warned by a number of fellow athletes that my mission of rowing clear across

America was a "mission impossible."

But I knew that I was *willing to pay the price,* and I wasn't ever going to quit! The following are memories from what the media dubbed "The Row Across America."

Pull, Rob, pull! I yelled at myself as I laboriously yanked on the handles on my RowCycle, a three-wheeled rowing machine. I would have to pull on the handles at least ten thousand more times merely to row over this one hill! It took four hours of pain to rack up only twenty miles in distance, and I had a staggering three thousand miles ahead of me. I was beginning to wonder how I ever thought I was going to make it, or if I would. Here I was, on the side of a mountain in the Mojave Desert. We were not only physically exhausted, we had almost exhausted our water supply. This early in my odyssey, I felt as if I were moving in and out of reality as I grew hypnotized by the incessant rowing and pulling on the handles.

Nothing but barrenness surrounded me; there was nothing but desert in every direction. The sun beat down on my brother Steve and I as the dryness and heat continued to sap the strength from our bodies. Steve rode a bicycle beside me and was packing seventy pounds of tools and extra water to boot. Although riding a bike was much easier than rowing, he nevertheless was sweating at the task. *Had I made a mistake in attempting this Guinness World Record for rowing?* I wondered.

Honk! Honk! A truck zoomed by and the driver waved enthusiastically at us. Maybe he'd heard about what we were doing. Steve and I felt slightly boosted by the trucker's encouragement and continued up the steep grade at over eighty pounds per stroke.

Pull, Rob, pull! I prodded myself again. I tried ignoring the pain I was experiencing in my arms, shoulders, back, chest and stomach. This was just the beginning; we would be surrounded by mountains literally for weeks. Finally the first day was over. We ate a huge meal and sacked out in our RV.

Power from on High

On the morning of the third day, Jeff, the third team member, woke us up at 5:30 A.M. and drove us to our starting place. On the way, Kristi (Steve's wife and the fourth team member) told me something I thought was a joke. "Rob, I had a dream last night you would be able to row eighty miles today." I just laughed.

"No, I'm serious," she continued.

"Boy, between being pregnant [Kristi was two months pregnant] and the pickle you ate last night, you were bound to have a weird dream."

She continued to explain her dream while I listened courteously, but I did not take it seriously. After all, after training for a year and a half for over twenty-two hundred miles, I knew my limitations. My record row for one day was sixty-four miles. That was in flat Fort Worth where I didn't even have to row the next day. Now I was in the mountains of California where I would have to row not only the next day, but virtually every day for the next three months. Eighty miles? It seemed an impossible dream. But the more I listened to her premonition, the more captivated I became with the idea.

Steve and I began the day by rolling down a hill. We were

thrilled when we realized that the trip into Palm Springs Valley was downhill for almost thirty miles. For over two straight hours, we managed to average sixteen miles per hour. It seemed as if the desert was brown death for as far as the eye could see. But finally we saw a patch of green on the horizon. Soon we reached the oasis ahead on Route 111, comprised of the cities of Palm Springs and Palm Desert, the only colorful views in sight. Everything else, although beautiful in a strange way, was brown and dead. We zoomed through both scenic towns so quickly that we lost track of time. When I looked down at my odometer, I was stunned to realize we'd gone fifty miles!

Soon we arrived at the point where we could finally go on the Interstate, or so we thought, and headed east. But there at the entrance, staring us in the face, was a sign that read No Bikes Allowed. There was also another discouraging sign as I looked up at Chiraco Summit as it disappeared into the sky. The sign read: Turn Off Air-Conditioner So Engine Does Not Overheat.

Just how long is this mountain? I wondered. The mountain had been there for millions of years. Now the question was: Who was going to win the victory today—the mountain or me? A policeman pulled over and guided us into Box Canyon.

He told us, "You will still go to the top of this mountain, but I can't let you ride on this stretch of interstate because there are runaway truck ramps up there and a truck may not be able to avoid hitting you if its brakes give out."

He led us around the side of the mountain and into the canyon for an alternate route. The first few miles were uphill but it was a small grade. Soon we were deep inside the canyon and the grade began to steepen to around 7 percent. However, the great thing about Box Canyon was that I could see only about a half a mile ahead. Since the road would turn and disappear to the right or the left each time, I didn't have to look twelve miles up as I would have if I had been on the interstate. A voice in my heart said, *Don't worry about the next seventeen miles. You can go half a mile, can't you?*

"Yes, I can go half a mile," I answered out loud.

That's how I continued through Box Canyon, a half mile at a time. At times, I would just concentrate on the next stroke. I began drinking a quart of water every other mile. I pulled stroke after stroke, mile after mile. I almost became comatose trying to escape the torture I was putting my body through.

I was jolted back to reality when a large lizard crawled across the road. Now I was fading in and out of consciousness as my heart raced and my muscles screamed. I watched as the miles slowly went by—seventy-five, seventy-six, seventy-seven. . . . An eagle soared overhead. I watched as it effortlessly followed the wind currents that carried him along. How I wished my path over the mountain was as easy! The miles continued to pass but much more slowly. My average speed at this point was three to four miles per hour, but I watched my odometer with growing excitement. Could it be done? Could I actually travel eighty miles today? My arm, back and stomach muscles cried out for me to stop this madness, but I couldn't quit now.

I realized this mountain was only a hunk of rock without a soul; its terrain was not a personal attack against me. Looking at my odometer after each half-mile stretch of road, it read: 78, 79, 79.5, 79.9. Steve went ahead to mark the spot, so I would have a clear stopping point. At this point I knew if I stopped short of eighty miles, after getting so close to it, I would feel that I wouldn't be able to start again. Suddenly, a chain broke on the RowCycle and almost immediately my muscles began to freeze up. The mountains seemed to laugh at me as I came just one tenth of a mile short of my goal. Knowing I could not wait for Steve to fix the chain, I began pushing on the wheels. The mountains stopped laughing (just hunks of rock!). Ten more pushes on the wheels, nine more, eight more. My body could not go on, yet it did. Five more, four, three, two! With one last surge of energy, I pushed the wheels one last time to the eighty-mile mark.

Jeff, Kristi and Steve erupted into cheers as we saw Kristi's impossible dream come true. My surroundings seemed almost surreal as my senses began to return. I cheered as best I could, barely able to raise my arms. I heard a high-pitched sound and looked around for what was causing it. Looking straight up I saw huge power lines and towers. The eighty-mile mark was right beneath them. The sound I heard was electricity surging through the wires. To me, it was as if God was saying, "Rob, you received power from on high to do this. You tell all of those churches out there that I did this."

Checking the altimeter, we realized that we had climbed from 183 feet below sea level to 1,425 feet above sea level in only twelve miles. I was ready for a gigantic meal. We drove back to Indio where we stayed at one of the most beautiful RV parks I had ever seen, emerging from the desert like a tropical oasis. This was an expensive place and I knew I was paying the bills, but I had to celebrate. After eating a multicourse meal, I relaxed in a hot tub. I made a few phone calls, read my Bible, then fell fast asleep and began dreaming about the following day. I was secretly praying no one would dream about how many miles I was supposed to go, since I wasn't sure I could ever top this day.

One of the requirements of the Guinness organization to achieve record recognition was to mark the road at the end of the day with a can of spray paint, so we could begin again at that exact mark the next morning. So we decided we were going to spray one letter of the name Jesus each day. The trip across California was supposed to take seven days, but because of the eighty-mile day and two sixty-mile days, we crossed California in five days. There are five letters in the name JESUS. In other words, Jesus took us across California, and I was convinced He would take us across the United States. Jeff stayed for another week but left us as we neared Phoenix. At the time, Jeff and I thought that his part of the Row Across America was over. However, over two thousand miles later I would be very surprised at what Jeff would be willing to do for me!

Rob and Steve pass through rocky terrain.

Rob and Steve ascend Chiraco Summit in California.

The Living Water

As we were passing through Arizona, we were separated from the RV for several hours. Kristi was almost three months pregnant and needed a nap. We were beginning to worry because we were getting hungry, but more importantly, we were low on water—*very low.* Suddenly, we heard Kristi on the radio.

"I see you. I'm about to pass. Everything okay?" Kristi asked.

"Yes, we're okay, but we need you to stop at the next exit."

Even though we were low on water, we knew we could make it to the next exit. We could see the next two overpasses up ahead and we were within a mile of them. We drank our last bit of water.

Kristi drove ahead. I looked at my odometer. It read forty-one miles. We could stop for the day at the next exit. We watched her pass the first exit. She didn't turn off. Why? We moved ahead, figuring she had used the second exit for some reason. Approaching the first exit, we felt a little sick. It was only an overpass, not an exit. As we looked ahead, we saw the second bridge was also an overpass! Steve called Kristi on the radio, but there was no answer. She was obviously over two miles away and out of range.

All right, don't panic, I said to myself. The next exit can't be far. But how much farther could we go without water?

Don't think; just row, I told myself.

Steve and I didn't talk. We just watched for the next exit as we started again. Somehow, knowing I was out of water and that I was sweating so heavily made me even thirstier.

Finally, we passed the second overpass and we scanned the horizon for the next exit. But the road just disappeared into the horizon. All we saw was brown sand and mountains. We looked at each other, then back at the road.

We began again without talking, knowing we had to save even the bit of moisture in our mouths. Then between the two overpasses we saw a sign that read: Gas and Lodging Next Exit—8 Miles.

I hoped we were not hallucinating in the desert sun: eight miles!

"I'm sure Kristi read this sign and is on her way back," Steve said quietly, hoping for the best.

"That's true, but if she isn't, we're in real trouble. We're going to have to move ahead. If she does come back, she'll see us from the other side and come back. Besides, she doesn't know we're out of water!"

I kept repeating to myself, *Jesus is the Living Water. He can satisfy our need for water!*

Before long our sweating slowed as our bodies began running out of water. My throat became too dry to talk. I tried not to look at my surroundings; it only made me thirstier. Slowly my energy level began dropping. Within another mile my average speed was only six miles per hour. At this speed we would reach Kristi in another hour. We normally drank a quart or more of water per hour, and the desert air was sucking every ounce of moisture right out of our bodies. Excruciatingly slowly, the miles passed. I hoped I was not getting dehydrated—it could take me days to recover from dehydration, and I knew that I had to be in the seat and rowing again in less than twelve hours!

"Rob, there it is," Steve cried with a raspy voice.

Up ahead I could barely see the next exit. Steve got on his radio immediately: "Kristi, we are out of water and sunburned. Get two quarts of water and wet washcloths ready for us."

Suddenly, I had a burst of power. My average speed picked up to eight and nine miles per hour again, and I exited the interstate. We saw the RV in the distance. My odometer read 49.6 miles, and we retired for the day.

❊   ❊   ❊

Two weeks later, the terrain was relatively flat with a few small hills. The wind was from the south, then finally from the west.

All through the trip, Steve and I wanted to shoot a picture of the large whirlwinds filled with dust that blew by us from time to time, but we wanted a spectacular one.

When a whirlwind passed, we would comment, "Is it large enough? Nah! Not quite." This went on for days. Well, as the saying goes, beware of what you wish for. . . .

The wind was growing stronger when something really unusual happened. Suddenly Steve looked over his shoulder with an odd expression. *What's wrong?* I wondered. I started to look back when he hollered, "Look out!"

Just as I turned to look, a large sagebrush hit us from behind and rolled over us. It scratched both of us as it bounced from me to Steve. We watched it as it rolled off into the distance, propelled by the fierce wind.

Steve made the incident complete by remarking, "That was a close 'brush' with death!" Steve and I love puns so we continued with a flurry of puns for an hour.

Later, I watched another spectacular sunset with the mountains turning reddish brown. I sat outside for an hour praying when I realized the wind was picking up. It was almost always windy in the high desert, but this was becoming unusually strong. Then I noticed something large was building on the horizon, but I fell asleep wondering what it was.

It was very windy from the west. The "something large" continued to build on the horizon. This was the strongest tail wind we had experienced on the trip, so we didn't complain. Yet Steve and I kept a wary eye on the sky behind us.

After a full day of rowing, we stayed in Carlsbad with a man named Mr. Harper. I went with him to a barn to feed his horses. He commented that they appeared to be extremely nervous for some reason. I turned around, seeing something large from the corner of my eye. There, only a few hundred yards from us was a wall of sand hundreds of feet high. It looked as if someone had stood the desert on its side. I pushed my chair as quickly as possible toward the house. I wasn't scared; I wanted my camera! This was definitely the sand picture we had been waiting for. I had barely grabbed my camera and yelled for Steve and Kristi when the monster sandstorm was upon us. The Harpers thought we were absolutely crazy as Steve, Kristi and I stayed outside taking pictures of one another. The sand was so thick it was difficult for us to breathe. We made a dash for the house just as the worst of the storm hit. For the next two hours, the storm proceeded to sandblast everything in its path. Hail, rain and thunder followed it. We finally had our picture, or so we thought. It turned out the camera battery was dead so the pictures came out all overexposed. Mr. Harper later told us it was the worst sandstorm they'd seen in half a century.

In Life, There's Always
One More Hill

Days later, when crossing from New Mexico into Texas, Steve and I had problems as we began to mount the Hueco Mountains. The first mountain road was six miles long and I had to stop every half mile for a break. Saturdays were always the hardest because it was the fifth or sixth consecutive day for me to row. As soon as I cleared the top of the first mountain, I was really excited—until I saw it was merely the first of many. Each time when I thought I was through, there was yet another mountain. It turned out that there were seven mountains we'd have to climb, all one after the other!

That's when the little voice in my heart spoke again: *In life, there's always one more hill. It's a lie to say, "I'm on a financially difficult hill, so I can't meet my financial obligations right now." Or to say, "I'm on a work-related hill, so I don't have time for my family right now." Or even to say, "I'm on a lazy hill, so I don't have to work right now."* I realized the voice was telling me that being on a hill is never an excuse for being weak or giving up. If all it takes is a hill to stop me, I'm already beaten, because in life there is always just one more hill to climb. I have all the tools I need. I just needed to continue pulling on the handles. Soon I would be over the hill.

That night, we stayed with Larry and Dorothy Jones, a couple from El Paso. I told them about my difficulty in climbing the Hueco Mountains. Larry looked at Dorothy wondering if he should break some bad news to me. Then he decided I should know the truth.

"Rob, the hills you just climbed are nothing compared to El

Capitan. It is one of the steepest grades in New Mexico, with some of the worst crosswinds in America."

I couldn't believe it. How could it be worse than the Hueco Mountains? I did not have to wait long to find out for myself.

We arrived at 11:30 P.M. and parked the RV on the side of the road beside our start point. We went to sleep at 1:00 A.M. The wind blew against the RV all night, shaking it from time to time. The wind did not bother me because it would be a tail-wind and would actually cut my work in half. Little did I know what was in store for us.

Matters started off badly and quickly progressed to worse when Steve greeted me at the door with a sick look on his face. "What's wrong?" I asked.

He didn't say a word. He just pointed to a tree standing beside the RV. It was bent over from the wind. I looked at it with a horrified expression: It was bending the wrong way! The wind had changed direction during the night and was now a fierce headwind.

I got into the RowCycle as the terrific headwind proceeded to blast our faces with sand and dust. It was steady at twenty miles an hour with gusts over forty. We started at 7:45 A.M. I was about to be tested. How badly did I want to succeed? I rowed minute after minute, hour after hour into a terrific headwind that was getting stronger. I had no momentum. The average stroke was around 100 pounds, and going uphill was so difficult I grunted with every stroke. Sand and dust swirled in the air. Steve and I did not talk; we had to use our energy to outlast the elements. I became lightheaded as the pain grew intense in my arms, hands, back and stomach.

"Stop, Steve!" I finally cried. "I can't take any more!" Beaten men, we both crawled into the RV after six hours of effort. We had covered only eighteen miles. After lunch we took a two-hour nap, but I was incredibly tired as I climbed back into the RowCycle. We tried drafting behind the RV, but the wind was so strong if we got even three feet away from the vehicle, it would whip around the side and stop us in our tracks. I was worn out and beat down when at 4:00 P.M., I yelled I had gone to the limit. I looked at my odometer. After a grueling ten hours of rowing, we'd traveled only twenty miles that day. I was discouraged and frazzled.

"Boom!" went the thunder jolting me out of my sleep. Over and over, lightning lit up the inside of the RV like midday. "Wham!" went the wind as it threw debris against the side of the RV. I lay there not wanting to look outside. After brief periods of broken sleep, I saw the sun as it started to light up the horizon.

I prayed God would change the weather. He did! The temperature fell to thirty-eight degrees, the wind increased to over forty-mile-per-hour headwinds, and it began raining.

"Thanks God, but this is not what I had in mind," I said out loud. Don't let anyone tell you that God doesn't have a sense of humor. And here's a tip I learned from this experience: When you pray, be specific!

Still we rowed east, heading toward that dark, ominous object that loomed ahead: El Capitan. It was throwing everything it had at us. Who would have the final victory was yet to be seen. The headwinds bore down on us with a vengeance. Clouds covered the horizon and met the desert in all four directions. Steve and I were averaging three miles per hour as the wind beat us back. At 9:00 A.M., we stopped at a rest area. I sat outside in the cold and ate a snack. We started rowing again. The gusts of wind were getting stronger and the cold was causing arthritis-like pains in my hands. Cold water leaked through my rain suit and dripped down my sweaty back. Conditions were unbearable for our fingers, as we had to fix a broken seat clamp on the RowCycle gloveless.

I started again. Steve caught up with me later. The head-winds were now so fierce it was impossible to hear each other speak.

Just then a pick-up pulled behind us. A cowboy jumped out and hollered, "What in the world are you boys a' doing?" He obviously thought we were crazy.

"I'm rowing across America," I said, realizing just how crazy it sounded. He stared at us, then at the weather, then at us again. He was certain he had run into two loonies without enough sense to get out of the rain.

"Throw your stuff in the back of my truck, and I'll take you to the top. You don't know what you guys are in for up ahead. I hate driving up this mountain in a truck—much less what you boys are doing."

I explained this was a Guinness World Record attempt and we could not cheat by even one inch. After attempting one more time to convince us to join him, he climbed into his warm truck and drove away, shaking his head and throwing a "God bless you" our way.

We rounded the corner and saw what I thought was a wall. It was not. It was the road!

Then we spotted a sign. We could not quite make it out. It looked like it had been in a war zone. The sides were bent and paint was peeling off. It was actually shaking worse than we were. As we approached the sign foot by foot up the steep grade against the wind, we could finally read it. It declared: Dangerous Crosswinds.

Steve and I glanced at each other as if to say: No kidding!

However, we did not know that the mountain on the right side of the road was protecting us against those crosswinds and we hadn't seen anything yet. Just after we passed the sign, we were hit by crosswinds of up to *eighty miles per hour*. It was blowing poor Steve all over the road. I was much more stable, being closer to the ground, but I had to correct my direction with each agonizing stroke. Between the wet road and the hurricane-force winds, Steve was blown dangerously close to the road and passing motorists. Somehow, after half a mile of unbridled fury, we moved past the gap in the mountains, and the winds dissipated a little. Larry Jones had told us that several eighteen-wheeler trucks blow over every year. Now we could believe it! As we neared the top, the headwinds increased their attack, seemingly trying to stop us. The wind almost took on the quality of a living creature. It became the enemy!

Finally, we stopped at 2:00 P.M. The mountain had won the day. I looked at my odometer. In seven hours of torment, I had covered only twelve miles. As a matter of fact, in just two days we had fallen behind our targeted mileage by 47.2 miles. I had to average over forty miles per day in order to keep up with all of my scheduled speaking engagements. I looked up at El Capitan and vowed I would return.

Then a miracle happened overnight: The storm broke. The winds were back to a mere twenty-five miles per hour. I was rowing by 7:15 into a spectacular sunrise. The clouds were leaving. Steve and I had only one mile before we reached the top. Within twenty minutes, we were there. We had won! And to the victor went breathtaking vistas of Texas and New Mexico. We stopped and snapped pictures of the highest point we would go on the entire trip. We were well over a mile high for the last time on our trip, but larger challenges still lay ahead.

As I passed El Capitan, it seemed so peaceful, not at all the same mountain it had been the day before. We had won this time! However, the enemy would try to stop me many more times on the trip before the battle was over.

Beyond the Southern Rockies lie all *nine hundred miles of Texas.* We were very excited to be in flat West Texas, though. As I said, we were spelling the name "Jesus" every fifty miles, one letter at a time. Well, across Texas we could have spelled, "Jesus, King of Kings and Lord of Lords!"

The Second Half
Begins with the "Flag"

Days later, close to Shreveport, Louisiana, my dad and Jane (my stepmother) joined me. We were exactly halfway across America! The ground was much flatter, but I was exhausted as I continued to row. We crested the top of the hill and there they were: the RV, the marker and the halfway point of the Row Across America. I continued to pull on the handles until there was no strength left. Up ahead I could see Dad and Jane. I looked at my dad. Suddenly, in my mind's eye, Dad was not standing by the RV; he was standing on the top of Fort McHenry. I went back in memory to an event from my childhood that would change my way of thinking forever. . . .

"Bang, bang, you're dead!" I yelled.

"You missed," my older brother Mike yelled as he returned fire and ran for cover behind a huge 150-year-old cannon.

Mike and I were holding replicas of 1812 pistols and playing army in a real live fort. For a seven-year-old boy, there wasn't a better place to play army than Fort McHenry, Maryland. The old walls of the fort rose above us like mountains of rock. Mike and I ran up a flight of stairs out of the coolness of the rock fortress into the sunlight. Just then an elderly woman walked between us, and we both opened fire on her. At ages eight and seven, everybody was fair game in war. Suddenly, a shadow appeared over us, and we looked up to see Dad towering over us. He peered down at us with a strange look on his face. Was it sadness? Why was he sad?

"Boys, I'm glad you're having a good time, but I'm afraid you're missing the point of our visit here. Come with me, boys."

We reluctantly followed him (he was cutting into our playtime) to the top of Fort McHenry. He pointed to the flag of the United States of America flying proudly over the fort. The only thing I knew about the flag was that we had to say the Pledge of Allegiance every day at school. It was a huge flag (and was actually one of the largest flags ever made).

"Boys, there's a story behind this flag. We're going to take a trip in time together. Look behind you. That is the United States of America. The year is 1814. Washington, D.C., has been totally destroyed by the most powerful fighting force on earth—the British. Hundreds of Americans are either dead or homeless. Now the British are on their way here. Several American fighting men form a living blockade to stop the British from taking the fort by land." He paused. "Now, turn around and look the other way. That water right over there is the Chesapeake Bay. It leads to the Atlantic Ocean. British ships have blocked off the bay. The men in the fort are badly outnumbered and prepared to do battle on land and sea. Only a few hundred men are in the fort. But they promised one another they would fight until the last one was dead before giving up. The battle began with cannons and rockets. The situation was hopeless, but they continued fighting. . . ."

❋   ❋   ❋

My mind returned to the present as I crossed the halfway point with my brother, Steve, by my side. Dad was clapping. Dad was older and grayer. But to me he was as tall as ever. I turned to Dad and said, "Thanks for everything, Dad." He seemed to understand exactly what I was feeling.

The rest of the memory of Fort McHenry would return during a few tough times. I realized my strength came from my Heavenly Father, but my earthly father always gave me something to spur me on when I needed it.

Where's Dad?

As we passed through Bossier City, it rained so hard we could barely see. I put a rain suit on, but it was more trouble than it was worth. I was soaked. Between rainstorms, it was so misty and dark our visibility was drastically reduced. We were afraid of being run down before a driver saw us, so Steve and I had to keep an eye on our mirrors all day. According to the radio, tornadoes were in the area. However, Steve and I were like two kids, yelling and screaming and having too much fun to worry about mere tornadoes. It was time for some more fun. Steve and I assumed the personalities of two otters (wet and sly). Dad and Jane drove the RV to a suitable place for a lunch stop, and they radioed their location to us. We topped a small hill, and there they were on the other side of the four-lane highway. It was difficult to see them because of the rain and mist, but they were visible. They were right behind a crossover, so it would not be difficult to maneuver across to the RV. Just then, Dad's voice came over the radio.

"I see you, boys. We're on the left-hand side of the road. Can you see us?"

Steve and I looked at each other. Another game was about to begin—the "I-can't-see-you" game. Steve radioed back and said we could not see them. We continued along the road, pretending to be looking all around for them.

Dad was frantic! It was raining on his boys and they were lost! He gave us his position several times. He was across the four lanes from us as we passed, pretending to be furiously looking for him. Dad probably wondered how we had made it this far across America.

"Boys, you're passing me right now. Can't you see us?"

We kept on going right past him looking everywhere but in the right direction. Now, Dad was getting mad.

"You guys are blind! I'm right here. This is crazy!"

"Dad, I don't appreciate you hiding from us like this," I returned.

Now Dad was fit to be tied. We went almost out of sight as Dad continued yelling at us to turn around. We turned at the next crossover, and then practically ran into the back of the RV still claiming we could not see him. Dad finally figured out we were only kidding him, and he laughed for days about the incident. And he never again asked if we could see him.

As we ate, the rain intensified. We did not want to leave the warmth and comfort of the RV, but we could wait no longer. By 1:30 we were rowing again. I left my rain suit off and never wore it again. It was better to be drenched by the cool rain then be trapped inside the suit. Steve and I watched for funnel clouds. The downpours were so torrential, we could barely hear each other. The claps of thunder resulting from huge bolts of lightning were deafening. Several times, we saw the limbs of trees blowing in circles as circular winds developed. We should have stopped for the day, but the storm was too exciting to miss.

A large van pulled beside us, and the driver asked us if we wanted to come in out of the rain. I answered no and began talking about our trip as I sat there in the RowCycle and almost drowned. The driver pointed to the side of the van, which read First Baptist Church of Minden, Louisiana. I was scheduled to speak there, so the driver knew all about us. He offered us shelter one more time and then left, wondering what kind of crazy guest speaker was coming.

We stopped for the day at the bottom of a hill outside Minden with over forty more miles behind us. I could go no farther. We were wet, cold, tired, and—you guessed it— extremely hungry. My only solace was having Steve at my side. He had faithfully followed me for almost two thousand miles. What a brother!

One night I was taking a routine shower in an RV park bathroom. Leaning forward to wash my hair, I felt a burn behind my left ear. I leaned back and looked up at the hot water handle. Trickling down from behind the handle was scalding hot water.

My eyes followed the dripping water down to my left foot. It was directly under the scalding hot water. It was burned so badly the skin was blistering up and falling off. It was a second-degree burn! The top of my foot looked more like raw hamburger meat than a foot. I immediately pulled my leg back and washed as quickly as I could. Once again I wished that I had the ability to feel pain on my feet. If I could, the burn never would have happened. When I returned to the RV, I dressed the foot in bandages and we prayed it would not get infected. We faced a much bigger challenge right around the corner.

We passed through Tuscaloosa. The road there was so bad that grass was growing up through the seams of the pavement. It pounded on the axles and I prayed they would not break like they had in the desert from similar pounding.

Just before lunch, Kristi smiled at both of us, turned the RV around and drove back to Tuscaloosa.

"Steve, where is she going?" I asked.

"She just has a few errands to run," he replied quietly. We continued the rest of the morning and into the early afternoon. When we ran out of water, Steve bought some Gatorade so we could press on. Steve was always quiet, but when he didn't talk at all, I knew there was a problem. We were almost to Birmingham. On a break I asked one more time, "Where's Kristi?"

Steve looked down toward the ground with a tear in his eye. Fighting back his emotions, he bit his lip and then said, "This morning, when she woke up, she was bleeding. She's gone to the doctor to see if she's losing the baby."

I couldn't believe my ears. It seemed as though our worst fears might become tragic realities. The rest of the day while rowing, I prayed, "Please don't let Kristi lose the baby!"

Had I pushed her too hard? Did I make a mistake by

allowing them to come on the trip with me? Steve and I wept as we continued as quickly as possible to a phone to call the hospital. Steve called and discovered that Kristi already left the hospital. We exited Highway 11 and proceeded north on the Interstate as planned. Within half an hour, Kristi returned in tears.

"The doctor said that the baby is close to a miscarriage. In his opinion, I should go home immediately and see my doctor. He also said I should stay in bed."

We stopped at mile marker 100 and drove to Tannehill State Park. Steve bought a ticket for Kristi to fly home the following morning.

In the meantime, I called Wanice. She was understandably upset about the baby and also had not planned on leaving home until our arrival in Washington. This meant she was going to have to drop everything and come running. After a brief discussion, we planned for Steve and me to go ahead alone until Wanice arrived a week later. I was on my way back to the RV to tell them about Wanice's plan to join us. Steve met me on the trail. He was completely broken when he confessed, "Rob, I want to go home, too. Kristi needs me."

I knew he was right. His first responsibility was to his own family. This meant I would be stranded at the RV park for a week waiting for Wanice to arrive. I had food and water. However, this would throw off all of the speaking engagements, not to mention forfeiture of the Guinness World Record. While I knew Steve had to go, he was security for me. Every time I was in trouble thus far, Steve had been there.

But that still, small voice in my heart said, *Let him go. Do you trust in man or in me?* I realized this was a time for me to

"Rest in the Lord, and wait patiently for Him," as Psalm 37:7 says. This message is repeated several times through the Psalms, including in Psalm 27:14: "Wait on the Lord; be of good courage, and He shall strengthen your heart."

I called Wanice back and told her I was going to be stranded, and she began to cry. But I hastened to reassure her that I was never alone, no matter what.

"Wanice, I've been telling churches all across America that if God is with us, no power can stop us. Well, it's time to see what we really believe." She agreed with me and called as many friends as she could to begin praying. Friends and relatives from coast to coast were praying for Kristi and her baby and for me. I was about to watch God go to work. I took a bath in a real bathtub in the park restroom. It was the only easy bath I had taken since leaving California. I realized I had not eaten since breakfast, over sixteen hours ago. After the bath, Steve fixed a bite for us to eat.

I called Wanice back at midnight to tell her goodnight and remind her not to worry too much; it would all work out in God's time. When she answered, she was crying again. But this time it was tears of joy.

"Rob, you're not going to believe this! Don Bright lost his job two weeks ago, and God promised him the reason would be revealed right away. As soon as I called, God verified in his heart that this was it. He'll be there in two weeks and ride the rest of the way to Washington with you. I'm also coming in two weeks. We'll meet you in Nashville. Gary Leroy just happens to be flying to Nashville in two weeks, and he's going to drive our car back! Also, Bob Peterson is flying in for the last week before Washington to help me."

"That's incredible, but what about the next two weeks?

How do I get to Nashville? I can't row two weeks all by myself."

"Rob . . . " she paused and began crying again. "Jeff Wilson is coming tomorrow. He's giving up another two weeks of vacation for you. He'll be there at 5:00 P.M. Rob, two weeks ago, Jeff felt he was supposed to cancel these next two weeks of meetings and traveling. He didn't know why until I called. He's leaving so fast he'll have to tell his boss why later."

I couldn't help thinking when Jeff helped me over two thousand miles ago that this was the reason. He was fully trained in our procedures and had the next two weeks free. Was this a coincidence? I didn't think so! In fact, I believe that when coincidences happen, it's just God working anonymously.

I didn't know what to say to Steve and Kristi to ease their pain. I thought about telling them about all of my friends coming, but it seemed callous to talk about the trip in light of their problem. I wrestled with guilt. Had I pushed Kristi too hard in her condition? One of the most important things in Steve's life was his family, but I recognized he was disappointed he could not finish the trip. I arranged for a police escort for Steve and Kristi to the airport the next morning. The police were also going to help me until my friends began arriving. Steve had ridden his bike twenty-two hundred miles at my side. Kristi had driven the RV that many miles and had cooked, done wash and everything else she was asked to do. Now the trip for Steve and Kristi was over. Or was it?

Steve woke me at 4:00 A.M. to tell me good-bye. It was as if I was looking into the eyes of a thirteen-year-old brother. I was transported back in time to our childhood, me just eighteen and heading off into the "wild blue yonder" of the air force. Steve and I had always been close. We depended on each other daily after our parents' divorce. We were always there for each other, but now I had to leave. I had said good-bye through tears. I felt as if I was abandoning him when he needed me most.

Steve tried to ease my conscience by saying, "Rob, you don't have a choice. You have to go. I'll be okay." Even so, Steve didn't learn until much later that I carried the guilt of that moment with me.

Suddenly, I was back in the present. Except now the roles were reversed. This time Steve had to leave. He could only say, "I'm sorry."

It was my turn to ease his mind. I repeated what he had told me seventeen years before: "Steve, you don't have a choice. You have to go. I'll be okay."

The police escorted Steve and Kristi to the airport. I watched the car drive out of sight. They were gone, and the RV was quiet and lonely. Everything I looked at reminded me of Steve and Kristi's sacrifice. I decided I was going to finish for all four of us—the baby, too! Nothing was going to stop me short of death! I finally fell asleep for three and a half hours.

During the short night I kept wondering, *Is Kristi going to lose the baby? Is it my fault?*

Finally, rising at 6:00, I crawled outside to my wheelchair and went to the phone. The only person I could think to call was David Allen, the pastor of Shiloh Baptist Church, where I had spoken just two days before. I told him about my situation, and to my great relief, he responded immediately, "Brother, I'll be there in one hour."

Within an hour, he arrived to drive the RV, having dropped his whole schedule at my call. He followed me all day while I rowed and even picked up Jeff at the airport. In the days to follow, my friends began arriving and I started feeling more secure again. My new team was composed of Don Bright, Wanice, and my two sons, Jason and Jonathan.

As always, Wanice was my biggest cheerleader, but to this day she says the prospect of ever spending any more time in an RV has absolutely no appeal to her whatsoever, no matter how luxurious the model. I can't blame her. While I was rowing frantically each and every day, trying to rack up the miles, then making my speaking engagements at night and on Sundays, she was trapped in the RV with two rambunctious, competitive siblings, ages ten and seven years old. Either that, or she was waiting by the side of the road someplace with them, trying to keep them fed, clean and, toughest task of all, entertained. Then of course I relied on her to keep track of my speaking schedule on the road, shop for food and feed us, and keep things organized in the RV. "I'm glad we did it," she says today of her eight weeks on the road with me rowing across the country, "but I wouldn't want to do it again!"

Weeks later, I was going up a hill and approaching a bridge. There was a car parked on the side of the road. As I passed it, a lady stepped out and yelled two words, "Home coming!"

I wondered what type of word association game we were playing, so I hollered back, "Football game, pom-poms, cheerleaders . . ."

"No! Home *coming!*"

I thought this person needed psychiatric care so I started again. I was halfway across the bridge moving uphill at a turtle's pace, when she screamed at me again, "Home coming!"

Still puzzled, I turned to look at her again and that's when I saw it. Right behind, barreling toward me was a house being moved on a huge tractor-trailer. Suddenly, I understood what

"Home coming" meant. I grabbed the handles and thought I would break them off trying to row to the other side. I moved over just as the mammoth truck passed. I waved at the lady, and she waved back. She knew what she had been saying, trying to warn me of the approaching danger. I just didn't get it.

The Fever

While in Tennessee, I felt extra tired. This should have been enough to tell me something was wrong, but I didn't take the hint until I developed a severe backache. I knew what that meant: a kidney infection! I took an antibiotic, but it was too late to stave it off. My temperature started to climb. I started rowing at 8:00 A.M. but had no energy and was growing sicker by the minute. My legs began to spasm as my spinal cord swelled with the rising temperature. The pain was like sticking my toes into a wall socket. But I persisted in rowing. I was compelled to continue. I couldn't quit! My boys were with me and I wanted to be the best example to them that I could be.

We passed by Abe Lincoln's birthplace, Hodgenville. Don and I stopped for a few minutes and looked around. Wanice took the boys for a long tour. But I was becoming sicker. We went down a four-mile-long winding hill and rowed by the "knob hills" Abe Lincoln had talked about. As we went over the hills, I wondered if the Appalachians would be this steep. I hadn't seen anything yet!

We finally caught up with the RV at 12:30 after thirty-three torturous miles. I crawled into the RV and climbed into bed, too sick to even eat. I began to sweat and shake. Within minutes I was shaking so badly with cold chills I was almost in convulsions. As my temperature rose, my legs began to be so hypersensitive that I literally screamed in pain. Wanice covered me with a blanket as I shook with fever. I lay there for two hours in 100-degree heat and humidity, yet I was so cold I was under two blankets and still shaking. As the minutes passed, my condition worsened.

Jason and Jonathan were sitting beside me as I sat up. I stared at the next mountain with an intense, stern look in my eyes. I knew the mountain stood between my dreams and me. Jason and Jonathan (ten and seven years old) were becoming very concerned for me.

"Dad, are you thinking you can't make it because you're sick and the mountains are so big?" one of the boys asked.

"No, boys. I was thinking there is no mountain too high, if God gives a man a dream! I'm also thinking of you two boys."

"What do you mean, Dad?"

"When you boys face challenges of your own, you'll remember this day. It will help you accomplish your goals," I said with a tear in my eye at the thought of continuing in this condition, yet I knew I had no choice.

I set the blankets aside and crept back into the RowCycle. I began rowing again by three o'clock. I had to go seven more miles to stay on schedule. Then I hit a three-mile hill. It was small, but it felt like a mountain to me. As my temperature rose, I was fading in and out of awareness. I began to cry with pain and was completely soaked with sweat. My mind was no longer rowing. It was back in time listening to my father high on top of Fort McHenry. . . .

❧   ❧   ❧

"Boys, the Americans were trapped both by sea and land. A few more men arrived to help protect the fort, but they were badly outnumbered. The men knew they could not win, but they fought anyway. They were prepared to die to keep the flag flying. The battle began. The British attacked the American Forces just southeast of Fort McHenry. Next, they attacked by sea. Fourteen hundred to eighteen hundred bombs hit Fort McHenry from the British ships. Men were dying inside and outside as the attack continued. The Americans fired back and yelled, 'We'll fight to our deaths to keep the flag flying!'"

❖   ❖   ❖

The memory faded, but my mind was still half there and half in the present due to the fever. "Keep the flag flying! Keep the flag flying," was my battle cry as I fought the sickness and suffering.

"What? What are you saying?" Don asked as he rode his bicycle next to me.

Realizing I was talking out loud, my mind came back to the present as we began to go down a two-mile-long hill. I had gone over forty-three miles for the day. I pulled into the parking lot, crawled into bed and continued to shake. One of my boys came over to me and said, "Dad, I'll never quit again!"

"Son, I'll be proud of you no matter what. But the only way you'll feel good about yourself is if you do your best. Whether you accomplish everything you try is not as important as trying your best. If you try your hardest, you have nothing to be ashamed of. Besides, as you climb the mountains in your life, I will feel good knowing I helped show you the way."

If nothing else good happened on the trip, it had been worth it. I was teaching my sons that with faith in God and the proper attitude anything is possible.

I shook all night with fever. I continued on the antibiotic and we all prayed for the infection to heal quickly.

The local media met us at 8:00 A.M. I was very sick and tired, but I began rowing by 9:30 when the police escort arrived. We passed through Bardstown, Kentucky, went across a narrow bridge and up a hill with no shoulder. I became awfully dizzy from the lack of food. Because I felt too sick to eat, I lost five more pounds (mostly muscle).

My legs continued to spasm badly, and I grunted with every stroke, but the fever finally started to drop. It was my third day of fever so I was very weak. I drank close to a quart of water every half hour because I was sweating so much. Don told me about his adventures on bike trips he had taken, and it gave me courage. Don wanted to help me row, but he knew he couldn't. I had to do it all myself. The steep hills and winding roads had little or no shoulder, so I had to focus.

The fever finally passed, but the next challenge was just around the corner. With fourteen weeks and ten states behind me, I still had three weeks and three states to go. The finish would have to come from the heart because that was all I had left.

The Wipeout

We were only five miles from Wheeling, West Virginia, when we went down a four-mile-long hill. I reached a speed of thirty-five miles per hour. In downtown Wheeling, Don and I crossed several huge suspension bridges. They were tremendous engineering achievements. Hills surrounded us in every direction and appeared to be straight up and down. Twice local media stopped me, and a network appearance was scheduled. One of the reporters warned us about Wheeling Hill. It was a 10 percent grade going up and the same going down. The trip up was tediously slow, and I broke a cable and spring because of the pressure on the row arms. The pressure per stroke was over one hundred pounds and I had to pull on the handles twelve hundred times to get up the steep grade.

We finally went over the top and began our descent. I was moving over forty miles per hour for the first time on the trip and finally slowed to thirty on a slight grade. We rounded the corner when I saw it: A manhole cover rose above the smooth road. I began braking and slowed to twenty-five when I hit it. I began careening wildly out of control. Everything slowed down. My back wheels came up off of the pavement one at a time as the RowCycle swerved out of control. Suddenly, I flipped over. My head hit the pavement so hard it cracked my helmet almost in two. My ears rang and my head was pounding. The RowCycle flipped once more, and I began sliding on my back. The road was ripping the skin right off my back, and there was nothing I could do about it. My right leg came out of the foot strap, swung wildly and hit the pavement, breaking a toe. Sparks flew as the metal on the side of the RowCycle scraped the road. Finally, the RowCycle came to a stop and so did I, as my shoulder hit the curb.

Two men named Tom and Gene jumped out of their car, and a policeman stopped to direct traffic. Don, Tom and Gene reached me as I was trying to sit up, but my head was reeling, and I couldn't regain my balance even to sit up. I looked at the RowCycle. The frame was bent and cracked. Almost every chain and cable was broken and torn. The American flag that was tied to the back of the RowCycle was on the ground. The sight of the flag and my pain caused me to travel back in time to another American flag. In my mind's eye I saw Dad towering over me once again on the top of Fort McHenry. . . .

❊ ❊ ❊

"Boys, the battle continued for two days. The American losses were extremely low so the British increased their attack. The ships pulled closer and began blowing the fort apart. Men were dying and ships were sinking as the battle raged on through the night. The American land forces fought so hard and killed so many of the enemy, the British troops moved back. Meanwhile, the British captured a man named Francis Scott Key. He watched the battle with horror from the ship. During the day, he knew the Americans were still fighting because he could see the huge American flag flying bravely over the fort. But during the night, the only time he could see the flag was when a bomb burst in the air near it. He watched helplessly as the British continued to dismantle the fort. Boys, listen to the words of the second verse of 'The Star-Spangled Banner.' It's more of a prayer than a declaration. It says if men are fighting for what is right, then God surely has to help them. Suddenly, during the middle of the night, the battle was over. The British dispersed in every direction. But who had won? It was pitch black, and Key could not see the flag. The smoke from burning ships was so thick he could hardly breathe. He held his breath waiting for the sun to rise. Whose flag was flying over Fort McHenry? . . ."

✣ ✣ ✣

I was back in the present looking at the American flag crumpled on the ground by the back of the RowCycle.

I crawled over to the flag and picked it up. "I'll keep it flying, Dad," I whispered.

I saw Wanice running to me. I had difficulty focusing my eyes, and everything still seemed to be moving in slow motion. Don and Wanice put the RowCycle on the back of the RV, then lifted me into my wheelchair. Tim, Gene and the policeman led us to the hospital. The doctor told me I had a mild concussion, a broken toe and a deep puncture on my right leg. I had scraped my arms and shoulders and had a large bruise on my right shoulder. It hurt so badly I could hardly raise my right arm. But most painful was the ripped skin on both shoulder blades. I was raw and had major road rash. The doctor told me I needed immediate medical attention and that the burn on my foot from weeks ago was infected. I realized this damage to my body was going to cause agony on each stroke. The thought of moving my arms and ripping the skin on my back was almost more than I could bear. How was I going to row now?

I was going to have the next two days off. I was about to leave for Denver on the only planned excursion of the trip. This would give Don two days to rebuild the RowCycle and me two days to heal. Sure, I had a mammoth excuse for quitting. But the memory of the men at Fort McHenry spurred me on. I was going to finish or die! We drove to Indian Springs State Park. I lay in bed wondering where the strength for talking and autographing books the following two days in Denver was going to come from. But the experience was great—I met booksellers and buyers from all over the world. The food was good, and the hotel bed was even better! I ate and slept for two glorious days and even better—no rowing.

The Spirit Wins

Days later while in the Appalachians, I was rowing over one of the seven ridges, and my body began yelling for me to stop. It tried to reason with me as if my brain was a separate entity. My body and brain talked with each other and my spirit stepped back to listen. My whole being hurt so fiercely that my body, soul and spirit seemed to be three separate people. I just listened in as a fourth party as they talked, barely conscious of my surroundings. My body spoke first.

"Look, I said yes when you wanted me to continue through twelve hundred miles of desert, over the Guadalupe Mountains against terrible headwinds, through rain, heat and cold. I said yes when you asked me to continue with little or no sleep, when you were stranded in Birmingham, even when you had a health-threatening kidney infection. I said yes when you wanted me to continue to row after the wipeout and over the first five ridges of the Appalachians. Now it's your turn to say yes when I ask you to stop. I can't do this anymore. I'm drained. If I have to, I will shut down on you."

My brain was next: "I have always taken care of you. I have trained you well for this. Besides, I am only asking for another week of effort. I will give you the rest and attention you need when you are done, but right now I need your support. Rob just wants our help a little bit longer."

My spirit was not sure who was going to win the argument. My body complained and continued sending messages to my brain. My brain ignored the pain and was immovable.

Suddenly, my spirit interrupted, "Didn't God deliver David from certain death when he faced Goliath? Didn't God deliver Gideon from certain death as he faced tens of thousands of the enemy with only three hundred men? Didn't God deliver Paul from certain death time after time on his missionary journeys? Surely God can get the three of us over this little-bitty mountain!"

I continued to row, waiting to see who was going to win the argument. I found myself sounding out words of praise. At first it was from my spirit alone. Soon my brain joined in, and finally my body shrugged its shoulders and agreed. This continued all the way up the side of the mountain. We were together again as praises flowed.

The Finish

July 30, 1990, was on the final day of the Row Across America. I looked at my watch. It was 11:15 A.M. We had to travel from Northeast Seventeenth Avenue to First Avenue, then back to Northwest Seventeenth Avenue in just forty-five minutes. It was almost the lunch rush hour, traffic was bumper to bumper and we did not have a police escort. We hit construction at 11:35. We prayed for a police escort, and one showed up for a few minutes—long enough for us to weave through the rest of the construction without stopping. We took a left on Northwest Seventeenth Avenue and passed the White House. Incredibly, we hit more construction. It was 11:45. We were directed to the west. My biking partners began stopping traffic for me using their bodies as human shields.

We arrived in the Mall area. It was 11:50, and we had almost two miles to go through dense crowds of people. Jeff was stationed at the Capitol with a radio and contacted us for the first time.

"We're waiting for you in the lawn behind the Capitol. There is quite a group waiting for you here. You need to take the ramp around to the back of the Capitol. Where are you?"

Don answered, "We're over a mile away from you, stuck in the crowd. We're coming as fast as we possibly can."

As the team continued to block the way for me, the memories of the trip began coming back to me. I thought about the mountains in the first three states; crossing twelve hundred miles of desert; El Capitan; nine hundred miles of Texas; the rain, hail, cold and wind; the fever in Kentucky; the wreck in Wheeling; and finally the Appalachians. I was so thankful that no matter what hell had thrown at me, I had depended on God and kept going.

A few people stopped me, asking if I was the one rowing across the country. Not having time to stop, I spoke while continuing to row. The bikers helped me through the crowd. I hit gravel four blocks from the Capitol. I pulled on the handles as hard as I could, and the inches passed by. I arrived at the front of the Capitol at 11:57. We passed several congressmen walking by, and they applauded as I climbed up the ramp around the building. On turning the corner, I saw Dad holding a sign of congratulations. As I looked at Dad, the final part of the Fort McHenry story came back to me. . . .

✤   ✤   ✤

"The battle was over. It was dark, and Francis Scott Key didn't know who had won. He waited the long hours until the fingers of the sun began rising up on the horizon of the sky. Slowly he could see the outline of the fort and then the flag. But it was still so dark, the flag was colorless. Slowly, as the morning sun rose higher, he could see it. The American flag was still flying! The small American force had held off the attack of the much more powerful British Army. Boys, when you face challenges in your life, I want you to remember these men. They died for your freedom so you could follow your dreams. When you quit, you make a mockery of their deaths. You are Americans. You don't have to quit in the face of adversity. Give it all you have, boys! That's all they did and that's all you can ever ask of yourselves."

As I passed Dad, I thanked him again, and he seemed to know what I was thinking and winked back at me. I looked ahead and saw the finish-line tape held by our two boys. Back in Kentucky, I had told them, "There is no mountain too high, no ocean too wide and no warrior strong enough to stop us if God gives us a dream."

Time stood still as Jason, Jonathan, Dad and I proudly looked into each other's eyes. My dad encouraged me while growing up, now I was encouraging them. We exchanged more love and admiration in that one second than some families do in a lifetime. I was running the race that God called me to run; now they could run theirs.

I passed through the tape. I had made it! I moved to the grassy area. My entire family was there, even Steve and Kristi, who was still with child (They were blessed with Katheryn

Marie on November 26, 1990.)! A senator and several congressmen congratulated me. I shared a few details of the trip with the press. I thanked my family individually by name and told how far each of them had come with me. It was over!

The Row Across America was honored with two entries in the Congressional Record, and two days later, the flag flew over the Capitol in honor of DynCorp and my family. I was presented a certificate of recognition signed by Arnold Schwarzenegger, chairman of the President's Council on Physical Fitness. I raised tens of thousands of dollars for paralysis research. Over the 120-day journey, I had spoken to over one hundred organizations, seventy-six of which were churches. In addition, we received a letter from President and Mrs. Bush congratulating us. Within the next few years, I received commendations from several well-known persons.

Family and friends rejoice at the finish.

Here are a few. Not bad for a guy who was told he'd never walk again.

Awards/Records/Recognition

President's Council on Physical Fitness, signed by Arnold Schwarzenegger.

Guinness World Record: "Rob Bryant of Fort Worth, Rowed 3,280 miles across the USA from Los Angeles to Washington, D.C., April 2 to July 30, 1990."

Honorable Roy Dyson, Congressman from Maryland: "Mr. Speaker, I rise today to pay tribute to DynCorp (Rob's employer) and to Rob Bryant. Rob Bryant has been a paraplegic since 1982 when he fell fifty feet from an oil rig. Despite his handicap, he has just completed a courageous 3,280-mile Row Across America. Mr. Speaker, it is both an honor and a pleasure to salute Rob Bryant today."

Honorable Pete Geren, Congressman from Texas: "Mr. Speaker, strength and perseverance rolled into town this week in the heart of Rob Bryant. He has just completed a 3,280-mile journey from Los Angeles to Washington, D.C., on a hand-propelled RowCycle. Rob Bryant is an author and stands tall in our eyes. He is truly an inspiration to all of us."

William Donald Schaefer, Governor of Maryland: "It is with great pleasure that I congratulate you. This grueling journey, which more than tripled the previous world record, is an outstanding and inspirational achievement. I hope you are as proud of your Maryland roots as we are of you."

Senator Charles Robb of Virginia: "Rob, it is with great

pleasure that I congratulate you for holding two world records and I am honored that I could greet you at the finish line at the Capitol. Congratulations to you and your family."

Bob Bolen, President of National Mayors Association, Mayor of Fort Worth, Texas: "Whereas Rob Bryant is an example of courage and unselfishness, I do hereby proclaim May 17, 1990, as Rob Bryant Day."

Annette Strauss, Mayor of Dallas, Texas: "On behalf of myself and the Dallas City Council, I do hereby proclaim Thursday, May 24, 1990, as Row Across America Day."

The Row Across America was officially a Guinness Record from 1992 to 2000.

EPILOGUE

It's been over a decade since I rowed across the country, and now we're in a new century as well. Have things gotten any easier? Not really, but that's the way life is and that's part of the challenge and excitement. I still keep up a very hectic schedule at work, church and with speaking engagements. Although my family is still my priority, both boys are grown and on their own in college. I've gotten better about a lot of things, like listening to my body and taking the hint to slow down to head off more serious problems. I've had more surgery, one that has helped prevent kidney infections, and I've had my gall bladder removed—no big deal.

Wanice and I had difficult times since my accident, but I'm happy to say that we will celebrate our twenty-fifth anniversary in 2001.

Jason is twenty-one and is a full-time student at Tarleton State University in Stephenville. His major is criminal justice/business. As a U.S. Marine Reservist, he works at the Ft. Worth Naval Air Station once a month.

Jonathan is seventeen, is on the varsity baseball and debate teams, is a National Honor Student, and was chosen to attend the Scholars Program in Houston at NASA. He has been voted as his senior class president this year. He has won many awards at school in academics and leadership. He is so busy with academics, yet still has time for church, baseball, friends and sometimes even his family. He received a congressional nomination from Joe Barton and is now attending the U.S. Naval Academy and hopes to become a pilot.

REACH OUT AND TOUCH SOMEONE

I was reminded of how blessed Wanice and I are to have each other and our sons when I visited the Telephone Baptist Church in Northeast Texas. On this particular Saturday night I stayed with William and Nelline Phillips, a retired couple who had actually built most of the homes in town. Their house was totally wheelchair accessible since their son was born with Down's syndrome and may eventually need it that way. We talked for over an hour and I noticed they didn't mention any grandchildren—highly unusual for couples their age. Then I learned that their oldest son could not have children, their middle child was killed in a hunting accident and their youngest son never married due to his retardation. I was sent to Telephone to minister to them, yet the Phillips family ministered to me— as well as to many of the youth in the church there that they have spiritually adopted as grandchildren. Through all this tragedy they are still devoted to each other.

IT'S NOT JUST A JOB . . .

The principles found in this book have also helped me achieve my business-related goals, beyond my dreams. Not yet forty-five years old, I am the vice president of Quality, Assurance & Compliance for DynCorp. There are three divisions of DynCorp, and I work directly for the presidents of two of them. In this capacity I travel around the world to locations where we maintain military bases and equipment for the U.S. government. I firmly believe that my career success is a direct result of hard work, determination and treating others the way I want to be treated (the Golden Rule really works), along with other principles listed within this book.

Some of the many places I've traveled to recently for work include: Bahrain, Bangkok, Bosnia, Colombia, Croatia, England, Honduras, Kosovo, Kuwait, Germany, Japan, Korea, Oman, Qatar and Switzerland. I also speak to local employees and churches on my travels when it does not conflict with business. I was on one such trip to Tegucigalpa, Honduras, in Central America. I had also been there one year before when Hurricane Mitch smashed into Honduras, killing thousands. Even so, this is one of my favorite trips each year. The country is beautiful and the people are friendly. DynCorp has a contract there to maintain the base for strategic defense and drug interdiction to the U.S. It is a very active base and some of our finest fighting personnel are located there.

My driver took me up to Soto Cono AFB, Joint Task Force Bravo (manned by army, marines and air force personnel) where I was to work all week. Mountains surround the base and the sunsets are spectacular. They teased me about my visit when it began raining on Monday night, since they blamed me for bringing Hurricane Mitch the year before. Then the rains came again on Tuesday and Wednesday night and washed out all of the bridges to the base except one. By Thursday it no longer seemed funny and they were all too glad to take me back to the airport. However, before I left, the base radio station advertised that I would be speaking on Wednesday at the chapel.

It was a terrific meeting and the chaplain, Captain Horton, is a wonderful example of Christ's love. But I figured that since these were seasoned Special Forces-type folks, the response to my message would be minimal. I was delightfully surprised when 100 percent of the men and women came forward to pray after I shared my testimony with them. Then I asked for someone to close us in prayer. The biggest, meanest-looking man in the room began to pray. He had tattoos everywhere, scars on his face and looked like a gorilla, not a man. But his prayer was one of the most beautiful prayers I have ever heard. It was as if heaven had opened up and this soldier had the key in his hands. The prayer was full of scripture, love and compassion. I saw something in his eyes that I had missed earlier when I was judging him by his rough appearance—it was the love of Christ. My mission to serve my company and Christ was accomplished. Allow your job to be a blessing to others, whether you drive a school bus full of kids, a garbage truck or a luxury sedan befitting a CEO. I don't see being a witness for Christ and doing my job as a conflict of interest; in fact, my religious beliefs enhance my performance.

One of the great things about my job is that I audit so many sites around the world that I can make suggestions concerning ideas that are working elsewhere in areas that may need improvement. There are two schools of thought when helping others improve (basically my job description). You can tell folks how messed up they are and only look at the negative, or you can tell them how good they are and then point out the few areas in which they need improvement. You can pump them up into being the employees you want them to be. Of course, positive reinforcement is a vital tool to teach children as well.

I work long hours, but sometimes the travel can be an adventure. I recently went to the Persian Gulf and almost to the Iraqi border. On a different trip I walked right through an ex-battle zone in Kosovo and Bosnia where the fighting between the Albanians and Serbs continues to this day. My Web site at *RobBryant.com* stays current with my round-the-world adventures.

One of the most exciting trips I have taken recently was to the drug-infested jungles of Colombia, where our company's mission is using military aircraft to spray and kill the plants grown in fields for cocaine. (And where they have the best coffee!) Bogotá is where our offices are, so I inspected aircraft, spraying operations, reports, procedures and processes there. I also bought beautiful emerald jewelry for Wanice (a happy wife means a happy family). Colombia is known for coffee, drugs and emeralds, and here I was, directly involved with all three.

However, the fun was just beginning. The next morning I said goodbye to the beautiful hotel for a three-day trip to the jungles of interior Colombia. I stayed in a small camp where I held classes for the employees to familiarize them with new quality and safety methodologies. I inspected the aircraft, records, maintenance and management. That night over a locally cooked meal of lentils, rice and beans, I met and talked to people for several hours, each of us slapping huge insects from time to time as they hovered around the lights—and us.

Later, I lifted weights with many of the big, strong search-and-rescue soldiers. They watched me curiously as I benched more than my weight (nothing for some of them). Around midnight I went to the perimeter of the camp with one of the Special Forces guys and we listened to the jungle. We heard the cries of almost a hundred types of birds, insects, lizards, frogs and animals (big cats like jaguars still prowl these jungles). Were Columbian guerrillas right there watching us? I didn't want to know.

It struck me as awesome that just a few days before leaving Texas, I spoke in Oklahoma, and worked in South Carolina and in Florida. Now I was in South America. I got a few hours of sleep and then flew out again. A few days later I stopped home, spent one-on-one time with each member of my family, then flew to a revival in Louisiana. Do I have a great life or what?

A strong work ethic will separate you from most employees in the world. But we need to balance our work life and home life. Too much work and not enough time with our families can be disastrous. For instance, just days after arriving home from an exhausting eighteen-day, six-country, thirty-three-thousand-mile flight trip literally around the circumference of the planet, I spent the Thanksgiving weekend with my family. I could have just crawled into a hole for four days since I was so tired, but I made sure I left energy for them. We can point to our bank accounts and large homes and expensive cars and say, "I did this all for you," but they won't be impressed. They want you and your time.

I am thankful for my family, job, this book, ministry and most especially for the positive attitude God has given me. I know I am blessed and am thankful for God's grace to this old sinner. May God bless you with determination and, more importantly, self-confidence. If an old paraplegic like me can accomplish the small things in this book, just imagine what you can do.

I wish you well as you overcome your own particular adversity! Just set the goal, visualize the steps, count the cost and then pay the price. Take the first step and then run like the wind. Even though I am in a wheelchair, I can still run the race. Even though you face adversity, you can overcome it and run the race, too! You don't have to be defeated by adversity anymore. You can do it!

Finally, never forget that God created us all as unique individuals, each special in our own way. We have our own abilities and disabilities. It is the adversity we encounter and learn to walk through that makes us strong. God gave you your disabilities to teach you to depend upon Him, and He will never give us more than we can handle. Remember His promise: "I will be with you always, even to the end of time" (Matthew 28:20).

ABOUT THE AUTHOR

Rob Bryant lives and works near Fort Worth, Texas, where he is the vice president of Quality, Assurance & Compliance for DynCorp, an aerospace company offering technology and solutions to modify government facilities and maintain military bases for the U.S. government around the world. After work and on weekends he spreads the word about Jesus Christ and tells his story of faith wherever he is invited. In the year 2000 alone, Rob spoke on three television programs, at thirteen high schools and four universities, twenty-four churches and visited thirty military bases, in eighteen U.S. states and fourteen other countries. At many of the events, especially where youth are involved, his speech ends with an impressive feat of strength as he "bench-presses" students and teachers. You can see what he's been up to lately and where he's scheduled to speak by going to his Web site, *www.RobBryant.com.*

Now that their two sons, Jason and Jonathan, are almost on their own, Rob is looking forward to having his wife of twenty-five years, Wanice, join him on some of his trips when it doesn't interfere with her job as a third-grade teacher. This is Rob's third book.

RECOMMENDED READING

Armstrong, Lance with Sally Jenkins. *It's Not About the Bike.* Putnam Publishing Group, 2000.

Carlson, Richard. *Don't Sweat the Small Stuff.* Hyperion, 1997.

Maxwell, John C. *The 21 Indispensable Qualities of a Leader.* Thomas Nelson, 1999.

Omartian, Stormie and Michael Omartian. The *Power of a Praying Wife.* Harvest House Publishers, 1997.

Ziglar, Zig. *See You at the Top.* Pelican Publishing, 1982.

The Holy Bible.

Your spouse's love notes and to-do lists.

All of your children's notes (frame them).

Discover the Power of Inspiration

In *Finding the Hero in Your Husband*, Dr. Slattery combines Christian principles, her professional expertise as a psychologist and personal experience as a wife in this indispensable book to help women improve their marriages.

Code # 9306 • Paperback • $12.95

Lena was born dreadfully deformed yet her parents refused to pander to her disabilities, encouraging her to enjoy life. *Footnotes* is a remarkable story by a one-of-a-kind woman who wholeheartedly believes that God her Creator never makes mistakes.

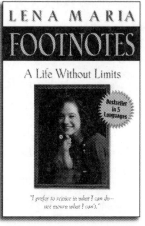

Code #911X • Paperback • $10.95

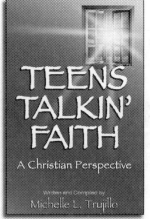

Teens Talkin' Faith is a gift from Michelle Trujillo and its teen contributors—a gift of faith, love and hope. Teens will accept it and hold it close to their hearts—it will make a difference in their lives.

Code #9411 • Paperback • $12.95

New from the
Chicken Soup Series

#1 New York Times
BESTSELLING AUTHORS
Jack Canfield
Mark Victor Hansen
Kimberly Kirberger

Chicken Soup for the **Teenage Soul** on **TOUGH STUFF**

Stories of Tough Times and Lessons Learned

Code #942X • Paperback • $12.95

#1 New York Times
BESTSELLER
Jack Canfield
Mark Victor Hansen
Marci Shimoff
Carol Kline

Chicken Soup for the **Mother's Soul 2**

More Stories to Open the Hearts and Rekindle the Spirits of Mothers

Code #8903 • Paperback • $12.95

#1 New York Times
BESTSELLING AUTHORS
Jack Canfield
Mark Victor Hansen
Jeff Aubery
Mark Donnelly
Chrissy Donnelly

Chicken Soup for the **Father's Soul**

Stories to Open the Hearts and Rekindle the Spirits of Fathers

Code #8946 • Paperback • $12.95

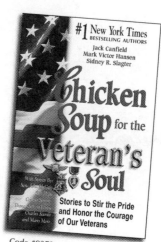

#1 New York Times
BESTSELLING AUTHORS
Jack Canfield
Mark Victor Hansen
Sidney R. Slagter

Chicken Soup for the **Veteran's Soul**

Stories to Stir the Pride and Honor the Courage of Our Veterans

Code #9373 • Paperback • $12.95

Available wherever books are sold.
To order direct: Phone 800.441.5569 • Online www.hci-online.com
Prices do not include shipping and handling. Your response code is BKS.

Celebrate Faith

#1 New York Times
BESTSELLING AUTHORS
Jack Canfield
Mark Victor Hansen
Patty Aubery
Nancy Mitchell Autio

Chicken Soup for the **Christian Family Soul**

With Stories By:
Dear Abby
Robert H. Schuller
Richard Lederer
Arthur Gordon
Penny Porter
Philip Gulley
Patricia Lorenz
And Many More

Stories to Open the Heart
and Rekindle the Spirit

Code #7141 • Paperback • $12.95

#1 New York Times
BESTSELLING AUTHORS
Jack Canfield
Mark Victor Hansen
Patty Aubery & Nancy Mitchell

Chicken Soup for the **Christian Soul**

With Outstanding
Contributions from:
Norman Vincent Peale
Corrie ten Boom
Dick Van Pullen
Charles W. Colson
Gary Smalley
Ken Wester Anderson
Dick Van Dyke
And Many More

101 Stories to
Open the Heart and
Rekindle the Spirit

Code #5017 • Paperback • $12.95

Available wherever books are sold.
To order direct: Phone 800.441.5569 • Online www.hci-online.com
Prices do not include shipping and handling. Your response code is BKS.